Tales of (

Other counties in this series include:

Tales of
Old Shropshire

~

Kathleen Lawrence-Smith
With illustrations by Don Osmond

COUNTRYSIDE BOOKS
NEWBURY, BERKSHIRE

First Published in 1991
© Kathleen Lawrence-Smith 1991

COUNTRYSIDE BOOKS
3 CATHERINE ROAD
NEWBURY, BERKSHIRE

ISBN 1 85306 141 7

Produced through MRM Associates Ltd., Reading
Typeset by Wessex Press Design & Print Ltd., Warminster
Printed in England by J. W. Arrowsmith Ltd., Bristol

Acknowledgments

I am indebted to the following for permission to quote from their publications:

Derek Hudson, author of *Munby, Man Of Two Worlds*, and to John Murray (Publishers) Ltd for extracts from that book.

Jacqueline Simpson, author of *The Folklore Of The Welsh Border*, and Publishers B. T. Batsford Ltd for the extract which I have quoted on 'Shropshire customs'.

Josiah Wedgwood & Sons Ltd for some details of 'The Coalport Story'.

The Rev J. H. Green, T.D. (Rector and Rural Dean of Hodnet) for information about 'The Hebers of Hodnet'.

Contents

CONTENTS

SHROPSHIRE: The map overleaf is by John Speede and shows the county as it was in the early seventeenth century.

Requiem For A Rake

IF ever there was justification for using the peculiar phrase 'spoiled rotten', it applies to the amazing career of Jack Mytton. In the year 1798 he inherited Halston Hall and the accumulated wealth of several generations of a highly respected county family. When he died in prison 36 years later, he had lost it all.

Nevertheless, Jack — by then commonly known as Mad Jack Mytton — was held in some regard by the townsfolk of nearby Shrewsbury. On the day of his funeral all the shops were closed and shuttered in respect, and church bells tolled in the nearby townships of Ellesmere and Whittington as well as at Halston itself. His strange, mad escapades captured the popular imagination and the tales told of him brightened many a dull day, added to which he had shown signs of spontaneous generosity to many of his contemporaries even when his wealth had become so depleted that he could ill afford it. Many of the local gentry joined the mourners in the churchyard, remembering the heyday of bygone Myttons to whom deference and honours had become commonplace and who had represented Shrewsbury in Parliament from time to time.

As evening fell on that cold March day in 1834, it is certain that in the taverns and inns along the road between Ellesmere and Oswestry, where the late squire had sown his wild oats as a boy, his perverse sense of humour would have been recalled with enjoyment — except, perhaps, by the victims of his practical jokes.

One of these had nervously expressed apprehension

when riding with Jack Mytton in a gig because of the lighthearted manner in which the young blood was urging on his steed to an ever faster pace. 'Have you ever been upset in a gig?' enquired his host, with a show of apparent concern. 'Fortunately, no,' admitted the passenger, to which Mytton retorted 'Well you have now!' as he swerved toward the bank which flanked the country road and deliberately hoisted the nearside wheel of the gig to a sharp angle up the incline. Over went the gig and both men were thrown to the ground!

It may be that Mytton was nettled at the implied criticism of his driving, as he had a considerable reputation for handling his horses with skill. He was a keen hunter and had once ridden his favourite mount, *Baronet*, into Halston Hall and spurred him on to scale and descend the grand staircase, to the consternation of the watching household. *Baronet* must have been a splendid animal. Jack Mytton would sometimes ride 50 miles each way to join a hunt in Staffordshire.

Perhaps it was his utter fearlessness which established his control over animals. He kept a bear at the Hall which he had purchased from a travelling showman and would entertain (and terrify) dinner guests by bringing her into the dining room and riding her around the table!

Rather more disconcerting, however, was his reaction to a boring conversationalist. Both were in a coffee shop at the time and Mytton had the effrontery to drop a burning coal into the chatterer's pocket! It was certainly effective. The victim flew outside to jump without ceremony into a nearby horse trough.

If only Jack Mytton could have contained his love of pranks within harmless channels all could have been so different and the financial ruin and disaster which brought such tragic consequences might have been avoided. He was not unintelligent. Far from it. Salvaged from an otherwise undisciplined and wasted education was a love of Classical writers. The works of Homer and Sophocles took root in his mind and surfaced at moments when all other sensible thought seemed to have been abandoned. He enjoyed success as a farmer, on more than one occasion winning awards at agricultural events.

Not once, but twice this goodlooking squire inspired romantic love, but any hopes that this would steady his mad gallop into ruin by reckless spending and heavy drinking were soon dashed. Sadly, his first wife died soon after giving birth to a daughter and though Jack grieved in all sincerity at this loss, he was not consoled by the child's survival and she was consigned to the care of others. Then Caroline Giffard, a relative of the Duke of Devonshire, fell in love with him. She was warned of his reckless ways but determined that her love would bring about a reformation. How his mother's hopes must have risen as he pledged himself to earn this lady's love.

But, alas, Caroline's hopes were dashed when his drinking again became uncontrollable. A man who breakfasts on a bottle of brandy and goes on to consume six bottles of port in the day is an unlikely prospect for married bliss. The company he kept and brought to Halston finally disabused her of any hope of salvaging the marriage and she sought to end it. His jealous claims, reinforced by the authority vested in the male sex in the early 19th century, prevented her from making a breakaway and resulted in her being immured in close confinement, guarded by one trusted servant. She eventually managed to get a cry for help to her family and was thrillingly rescued during Mytton's temporary absence from the Hall. The child she bore him, who was named as his heir, was passed to Jack's longsuffering mother for upbringing.

The departure of Caroline brought a further degree of recklessness into Jack Mytton's turbulent life, but it was probably his love of horses and gambling which put the final blight on the tragi-comedy of his career. What money he did not lose on gambling or reckless spending he gave away with prodigal abandon into bankruptcy.

Not even the sacrifice of his great home and contents could save him from the threat of imprisonment for debt in his mid thirties. He staved off the ignominy temporarily by a flight to the Continent and here an incredible act of folly almost ended his life. To cure himself one restless night from a bout of hiccoughs he set fire to his breast and shoulders! Now those who judged him insane were surely justified in calling him Mad Jack. The friend who later became his biographer was summoned to the scene by his distressed servant and was horrified at his plight. The servant had — for good or ill — saved his life by rolling him in a blanket.

He was brought home as soon as he made a partial recovery to face the settlement of his affairs and imprisonment at Shrewsbury for debts which could not be met from his remaining assets. Transferred to the King's Bench Prison in London, his life finally flickered out as a result of gaol fever. So came the last sad offices by his mother, to arrange the long journey home to Halston for burial.

His friend and biographer, C. J. Apperley, lays upon his mother's shoulders the blame for the years of outrageous behaviour and profligate living. If, indeed, his mother was to blame for spoiling him, she paid a heavy price for her folly, not once but over and over again before she reclaimed his body. One can only imagine the heartbreak and final despair which attended her on that last journey with her only child. The beautiful home he had inherited and all his wealth had vanished, but she found a place for him in the churchyard and may even have breathed a gentle sigh of relief that the long struggle to reclaim him was over.

It might well be thought that this was the last his native county would see of him, but a curious legend sprang up as a result of the burial party having to halt for the night at the coaching inn now known as the Mytton and Mermaid Hotel at Atcham. Here a rumour persists to this day that in addition to that pet bear he kept 2,000 dogs and 60 cats in Halston Hall, and moreover that his ghost roams the corridors of the hotel that had once seen him enjoying convivial company before he reached the sad point of no return.

Laughing Tam

THE bearer of bad news is seldom popular, as Thomas
Telford found when called in by the churchwardens
of St Chad's in Shrewsbury to advise them about their
leaking church roof. He had to tell the churchmen that the
roof mattered little because large fractures in the walls
rendered the whole building 'in a shattered condition'. It
was subsiding as a result of bad foundations, and grave
diggers had made the situation worse by digging too close
to the walls.

Telford was Shrewsbury's County Surveyor, who had
already earned a considerable reputation as a civil
engineer, yet his report was received with suspicion — and
an ill-disguised insinuation that Telford was exaggerating
the danger, so the Surveyor left them to their deliberations.
Three days later the building collapsed with a roar at the
first stroke of the church bell! Two chimney sweeps passing
by had an astonishing beginning to their working day, and
lived to tell the tale.

Writing to a friend shortly afterwards Telford described
the churchwardens' attitude '. . . these fractures were said
to have been there since time immorial [sic] — and it was
said by even sensible people that professional men always
wish'd to carve out employment for themselves: and that
the whole might be done at a small expense which they
proceeded to do — and I gave myself no disturbance when
lo and behold on the morning of the ninth inst the very
parts I had pointed out gave way — and down tumbled the

16

mighty mass — forming a very remarkable, magnificent Ruin!'

Telford's cheerful reaction to the contretemps recalls a faint echo of the boyhood humour which earned for him the name of Laughing Tam. He was born in 1747 in the little Scottish hamlet of Eskdale, his father dying only four months later. The shepherd's widow was poverty stricken and was obliged to seek a home with a relative, who became Tom's guardian. As the boy progressed through the village school nobody seemed to notice any outstanding potential in him, and all spare hours were spent working in the fields or tending the flocks of neighbouring farmers. He must have thought about the father he had never known but whose tombstone was to describe him as an 'unblameable shepherd'. Was this to be Tom's forte, too?

But, no. Tom's guardian (his uncle) apprenticed the boy to a local stonemason — and unwittingly set him on the first rung of a ladder to success, wealth and considerable fame. Even so, his skill would have been limited to good craftsmanship had it not been for the fortunate errand which took him to a Miss Pasley of Langholme, whose door swung open to admit Tom — via her library — into the wonderful, hidden world that lies between the covers of good books. He developed a taste for literature, discovered he had a talent for writing verse, but also glimpsed that in the rough material he cradled in his hands there lay a world of design and creative vision. When 24 years old Tom took the long, winding road to seek his fortune in London.

But London was not to be Tom Telford's Mecca. It was Shropshire which would witness, and enable him to realise, his full potential. Architectural skill which Tom had picked up came into play when the MP for Shrewsbury, Sir William Pulteney, met him in London and presented him with the challenge of turning the derelict Shrewsbury Castle into a home. Sir William, a dour Scot who was hard to please, was delighted with the result. As he settled into his country seat he promptly persuaded Shropshire County Council to appoint their first ever County Surveyor — and that Telford was their man!

The appointment proved of great mutual advantage as Tom progressed from architectural skill to civil engineering. His ingenuity produced well constructed buildings of lasting use (Shrewsbury Gaol, for instance), but he also found use for the neglected material lying in stone quarries in South Shropshire. He laid roads by what was then a revolutionary method. Over solid foundations he laid stones broken into fragments which became impacted with use and produced load-bearing surfaces. These were resistant to heavy rainfall in contrast to the quagmires which had bedevilled travellers and traders in the past. Many of these routes give excellent service today and would provide sufficient reason — even if there are no others — for the county naming their new overspill town, 150 years later, after this great practical engineer. But there were yet more strings to his bow.

When Roman relics were uncovered beneath farming land at Wroxeter, it was the County Surveyor who investigated and prevented what turned out to be the Roman city of Viroconium from being ploughed under. Very little interest was shown in archaeology then, but Telford's intervention proved to be vital and set the pattern for arousing public concern over preservation.

When a violent storm led to flooding and the destruction of an old bridge at Buildwas in the winter of 1795 Telford turned his attention to bridge building. Prompted by the beauty and strength of the first iron bridge at nearby Coalbrookdale, the County Surveyor designed and supervised the building of a single span cast iron replacement which met the need and greatly enhanced the scene. Then in the space of five years he built 40 road bridges in Shropshire!

Perhaps more spectacular than all, came the bridges

skilfully designed 'to carry water over water' — aqueducts built over rivers. These then formed part of the canal system which many feel to be Telford's finest achievement. Canals provided easy, reliable transportation for the heavy goods — iron, coal etc — for which the Severn Gorge was becoming famous. It is said that water transport halved the price of coal almost at a stroke, making merchandise highly competitive just as the Industrial Revolution was in full swing.

The most spectacular of Telford's projects in Shropshire must surely have been the design and construction of the Ellesmere Canal for which he was appointed Engineer in 1793. The prolific waterways in the north of the county were enhanced by this triumph of engineering. The area contains seven small tree-fringed lakes known as meres — Blake Mere, Cross Mere, Kettle Mere, Newton Mere, Cole Mere and White Mere, while the largest, which has the town of Ellesmere on its west bank, is simply known as The Mere — 116 acres fostering bird life together with boating delights for leisure hours and holidays. In this area the canal was constructed to link the rivers Severn and Mersey. To carry the canal over the Vale of Llangollen, Telford designed an aqueduct 125 ft high and 1,000 ft long. What a thrill it must have been to cross that vale in a vessel for the first time! Also, perhaps, an act of faith.

Thomas Telford's accomplishments spread far beyond Shropshire as his fame grew, and are too numerous to recount fully. But toward the end of his life (he reached the age of 74) he could look back without regrets and was even heard to say that it was an advantage for a man to be born poor! Even when he was not initiating new projects it was his pleasure to travel around Britain visiting the scenes of his developments and recording progress with keen objectivity.

After such a career it is fitting that the shepherd's son was honoured by burial in Westminster Abbey. But he

19

never forgot his origins, nor lost a love for his birthplace. In his will he left a generous sum to his old village church, to that of Langholme where he had spent so many happy hours with Miss Pasley, and made provision for a library to benefit schoolchildren. It is not surprising that his busy, eventful life never afforded him time for romance, marriage and fatherhood. His buildings, roads, bridges and waterways are the children which survive him and perpetuate his memory.

Up The Brown Clee!

FOR the hardworking quarrymen hacking away at the stony ground on the summit of Brown Clee Hill it was frustrating to watch the Industrial Revolution of the 19th century passing them by. Quarry owners were getting a poor return for their investment, and workers recruited from hillside cottages scratched a bare living at twopence an hour. Despite the rich yield of minerals to be found at the top of Brown Clee, output of iron, coal, copper, basalt and limestone was severely limited because the only means of bringing it down the rough hillside trackways was by packhorse or on the backs of labouring men and even of some tough womenfolk. Meanwhile, down at the foot of the hill, the Great Western Railway laid their line through Cleobury Mortimer in 1864 to carry freight, enabling other industries to expand.

The news galvanised local industrialists into action to push for a branch railway line to mount the hill to Ditton Priors at the top, with a return track to despatch saleable cargo down to the main line and out to waiting customers.

At last, in October 1900, a public enquiry pronounced in favour of the project. The twelve mile line was ready to take off . . . on paper! The approval sparked off great rejoicing and celebration among the promoters. But what a battle lay ahead! The struggle was to last eight more gruelling years, to outlive Viscount Boyne who was a moving spirit behind the plan and over whose land the track would run, and to bring tragedy alongside the ultimate triumph.

The sheer effort involved in laying a rail track up the hill —

at one point as steep as 1 in 4½ — was prodigious. To get the waggons up that incline, pushed by two engines from behind, was an engineering triumph, using heavy steel cables attached to brake waggons on the upward track to control the descending full loads on the downward one. The cables circled around a winding drum on the hill's summit.

But eventually negotiations with landowners, arguments with geologists, disputes with environmentalists, physical and technical problems and the demands of safety tests were all overcome. Even the general public became enthusiastic when it transpired that passengers could also be carried. The Cleobury Mortimer and Ditton Priors Light Railway was about to be launched.

Just what went wrong in the closing, exciting days of preparation, nobody was ever to solve satisfactorily. On a lovely May morning in 1908 Driver Jack Strong was at the controls of the first engine which was pushing two loaded trucks of equipment and ash up the hill, and Ben Revell was driving the second one. When the engines got 100 yards up the steep portion of the incline they ground to a halt and the drivers could not even hold the waggons still. There was nothing to be done but slowly retreat downhill to the gradient's starting point. For a second attempt one of the loaded trucks was disconnected and the ascent began again with the two engines pushing only one truck. Jack Strong's engine was in the lead, Ben Revell's following it.

Then the second attempt failed. They shuddered to a halt and the truck's weight began to push the two engines back down. The pull of gravity could not be overcome, even by thrusting the engine full steam ahead while also applying the brakes. The nerve-wracking experience of sliding helplessly backwards was the plight of both drivers for a quarter of a mile before the ash-filled waggon slid off the rails.

To Driver Strong's joy the engines remained upright. But when he looked around to share his relief with Ben Revell, his colleague was missing! Driver Revell must have lost his balance on the footplate and was found on the ground in the four ft way. Driver Strong's engine had gone over him.

A verdict of Accidental Death was returned at the inquest and the loss of a popular colleague threw a shadow over the final preparation for opening the line.

Soon the branch line became part and parcel of the South Shropshire scene and a spirit of bonhomie sprang up between railmen and local villagers. Two Cleobury men (W. Smith and K. Beddoes) compiled a history in 1980, published by the Oxford Publishing Company, of *The Cleobury Mortimer and Ditton Priors Light Railway* which beautifully recreates the sense of goodwill it generated as it collected and delivered more delectable goods than the material it sent down. Milk, flour, beer, animal foods, fruit and sugar beet were all carried in the waggons and a cattle train was run to and from Kidderminster market once a week.

Drivers would drop off seed for a farmer into the exact field where it was needed, and would throw off steam coals from their cab to 'keep the home fires burning' in war time for soldiers encamped along the route. A farm horse was hauled from a muddy ditch by an obliging locomotive driver, and it was a regular occurrence to pull up at a spot where no station platform existed to haul aboard an old lady who lived near the track.

The passenger services lasted for 30 years, by when petrol-fed engines and better road surfaces were encouraging other modes of transport. As the minerals along the hill top were worked out, so demand for the light railway's services decreased, and eventually Beeching's axe signalled its death warrant. An American army contingent in 1967 took over the territory at Ditton Priors, widened the road tracks with constant passage of vehicles, and thus provided an alternative route. This finally put paid to the nostalgic lobbying by rail enthusiasts to get this friendly little branch line reopened. The CM & D Light Railway had finally run out of steam.

'A Long Dark Man'

THIS must have been the worst moment of Charles
Stuart's eventful life. Crouching alone on a damp and
rotting tree stump in a woodland clearing in the dawn of a
September day in 1651, he started at the sound of snapping
twigs and of approaching stumbling footfalls. A moment
later he looked up into the anguished gaze of the Royalist
Colonel Careless, who struggled ineffectually to stem a
rush of tears at the sight of his weary, ill-clad, travel-stained
sovereign.

Tears are infectious. It is likely that the 21 year old King,
crowned with such hopes eight months earlier in Scotland,
was also struggling for self control. The two had last been
together three days earlier, amid clamour and confusion at
Worcester. It was Careless who had led the last hopeless
charge against swarming, exultant Roundheads as they
burst through the city gate. After that came the terse
command to abandon the struggle and scramble
desperately for the only remaining exit from the city. The
Colonel fled northwards to the refuge in Shropshire of
which, by happy chance, he had heard. For three nights
past, he had lain uneasily in hiding at Boscobel, not
knowing until now that Charles II had also eluded pursuit
and survived — but, alas, in such a state and in such a
predicament! The man who thought to reclaim a throne
now squatted awkwardly on a rotting treetrunk. The air
hung heavy with a sense of failure and fear.

It must have been a relief when the two were joined by
Richard Penderel, the young woodcutter from nearby

White Ladies Priory, who had brought about this reunion. Both were thankful when Penderel motioned them to follow him out of the wood and with him they covered the short walk to Boscobel, the black and white hunting lodge which was known to have sheltered many a Catholic priest during persecution. What joy and relief as they were welcomed to breakfast and to attendance upon the poor blistered royal feet while Careless listened spellbound to the King's account of his ordeal over the past three rain-sodden nights.

It transpired that following the disaster at Worcester, while the Colonel himself had been lying in comparative luxury in the cramped secret lair at Boscobel, the King had reached the home of the Penderel brothers — five farmworkers, known to be Catholics — who reacted swiftly to the sudden, fearful responsibility thrust upon them. The King's life was in their hands. It was a fearful, yet welcome responsibility.

Then, while the King sat to a breakfast of sack and biscuits, the brothers found him rough garments like their own, cropped the Royal locks and smeared the King with soot. Weary as he was, and because all nearby houses were being searched, the family urged him outdoors just before dawn in the guise of a woodcutter. Despite the pitiless downpour he had to conceal himself all that day in Spring Coppice Wood. Roundheads were swarming north in pursuit of retreating Scots soldiers, and it was dusk before the King could be conducted across the heath to the home of the Penderels' widowed mother at Hobbal Grange.

To try for refuge at Boscobel was tempting, but a good breakfast of bacon and eggs heartened Charles sufficiently to accept Richard Penderel's offer of guidance for an overnight dash ten miles westwards to the river Severn where, hopefully, he could cross to Wales and the coast to return to refuge in France.

It had been an exhausting, rainsoaked journey on foot and fraught with danger. By midnight they had reached Evelith but failed to creep by without attracting the attention of the miller who unfortunately chanced to be outside his front door. He hailed them, but Penderel and the King kept silent and fled by, spurred on by the sound of sharp cries as the miller summoned help to chase the silent unknowns who had refused to answer to his challenge. The fugitives ran until exhausted, lay in mud until the sounds of pursuit died away, then stumbled on to Madeley where, Richard declared confidently, Francis Wolfe would surely aid them. They arrived in the early hours of the morning, footsore and icy cold, only to learn that their exhausting journey had been in vain. Every river crossing was guarded by Cromwell's men. They had no choice but to return to Boscobel and seek another route.

The terrible disappointment was mitigated by the courageous kindness of Francis Wolfe and his daughter, who sheltered the King and Penderel in their hayloft for what remained of the night and the next day. The Wolfes smuggled food, money and dry clothing into the barn. Most welcome of all were the new shoes and stockings — sheer bliss after the rough tramp overnight when forced to kick aside ill-fitting shoes and finish the journey to Madeley in tattered socks. The rest in the barn had been a godsend, restoring them to tackle the return journey to Boscobel.

As darkness fell again they crept out to retrace their way over now flooded roads, and at one point it was Charles who had to rescue the non-swimmer Penderel. At three o'clock in the morning they were back in the woodland area near Boscobel, where Charles waited while Penderel went ahead to check the situation at the big house. Fortune smiled for the first time since the disaster at Worcester when Penderel found Boscobel temporarily clear of enemies, chanced upon Colonel Careless hiding there, and

26

brought about the emotional reunion between the Colonel and his sovereign lord.

What a boon that refuge at Boscobel turned out to be, even though the concealed sleeping quarters beneath the trap door of the cheese room were so cramped. During the hours of daylight the King and his companion were obliged to creep outdoors through the hidden exit in the chimney into the woods. It was here on that momentous Saturday following defeat at Worcester, that they found the famous hollowed oak in which to perch while Roundhead searchers beat hedges and undergrowth below. It is reported that the King fell asleep in the oak, supported by Careless's arm until the Colonel was forced, through numbness and fatigue, to cautiously arouse the sleeper. Meanwhile the faithful Penderels hacked around with woodcutters' tools, completely impervious to the proclamation offering £1,000 reward to any who would betray 'Charles Stuart, a long dark man, above two yards high' and threatening death to those harbouring him.

On the contrary, not only did the selfless friends refuse the bribe, but Francis Yates (brother-in-law to the Penderels) shyly came and offered the King all he possessed — 30 pieces of silver. How odd that the proverbial price of betrayal should have then sealed an act of deepest loyalty. (And how sad that his part in the escape later cost Yates his life.)

Boscobel provided a marvellous respite for the King. He awoke on the Sunday morning to the sound of church bells from nearby Tong, which he afterwards remembered with deep pleasure. Breakfast was brought and he was allowed out into the garden for a few blissful hours to rest his feet. Though caution was the dominant keyword, a new and hopeful mood had come with the news that John Penderel was travelling the eight miles to Moseley Old Hall across the county border in Staffordshire to seek help from a Catholic gentleman and his priest, Father Huddleston.

There, with the connivance of their friend Colonel Lane and his sister, was hatched the plot which was to set in motion the most famous escape in English history.

One last service was rendered by the Penderels to finalise those epic days in Shropshire. Because Charles's feet had not healed when dusk fell on that Sabbath night, his journey into Staffordshire was made astride Humphrey Penderel's old mill horse. The five loyal brothers and Francis Yates tramped alongside forming a guard, armed with concealed pistols, making for the meeting point pre-arranged with Father Huddleston, who waited for the King beneath a shadowed grove of trees. In all the years to come, including the Restoration of the Monarchy, the King was never better served than on that night of quiet darkness, moving resolutely over the Shropshire countryside.

Nine years later, in May 1660, Charles II was welcomed back to London with joyous celebrations. The Lord Mayor's Show processing through the capital featured a pageant which was greeted with a roar of approval. On a great wheeled platform was a reconstruction of the scene in Boscobel Wood. A spreading oak tree was the centrepiece with a figure unmistakeably representing Charles perched among the branches high above searching figures below. Charles had his faults and readily admitted them, but it has been said that his essentially human qualities set him apart from other sovereigns. Could it be that his experiences in Shropshire contributed in some measure to that saving grace?

The Unlikely Hero

T HE story of Robert Clive should encourage hope in every parent with an unmanageable child. Robert was born in 1725 to Richard and Rebecca Clive at Styche, an Elizabethan manor house near Market Drayton. He was only four days old when presented for baptism at the old Saxon church in the village of Moreton Saye.

No one could guess that behind that puckered little face lay a personality of amazing contrasts, or that he would drive his father to near despair when a toddler and throughout his schooldays. Perhaps today he would be diagnosed as hyperactive, or the victim of food allergies; he was subject to violent stomach pains from time to time. How his mother retained her love for him while bearing twelve other children remains a mystery, but for a few years Rebecca's childless sister relieved her of him. Before he was ten years old, the noisy, belligerent lad was back with fists flying at any provocation.

He was plucky, as the well known escapade on top of the parish church steeple at Market Drayton proved. Seated astride a stone gargoyle, high above the town, he laughed, kicked out and waved in sheer indifference to cries of warning and apprehension from onlookers below.

At school, though having little respect for lessons, Robert was leader of a boisterous gang who followed him into mischief, and even into a highly organised protection racket with local shops! His father was incensed at continuous complaints and harassed by lack of means to support his big family and maintain repairs in the 500 year

old damp and dilapidated home he had inherited. As local squire he had a reputation to uphold, but he was an unsuccessful lawyer, invariably losing his cases. However he sent his problem child to boarding schools, even for brief periods, and finally to study commerce and book-keeping.

This led to the offer of employment with the thriving East India Company and, in March 1743, Robert embarked on a hazardous, trouble-plagued 18 month long voyage to Madras. His father was unable to make the customary allowance for a lad in his position, and he was poor, lonely, unwanted, homesick, seasick and heavily in debt to the ship's captain when he arrived in India.

Ten years (almost to the day) after leaving England Robert re-embarked at Madras in the *Bombay Castle* to return home — rich, confident, married to a lovely lady and a national hero! After two desperately unhappy years (and two suicide attempts) there had occurred a chain of events which discovered hidden resources in this unpredictable youth. Shortly before his 21st birthday the French had attacked Fort St George where he worked, in an attempt to establish their empire in India. With a friend, Edward Maskelyne, Robert escaped custody, disguised as a Moslem, fled 100 miles to Fort St David and set in motion a train of events which repulsed the French, saved the East India Company from destruction, and made history. Without military education or connections he led an army with outstanding courage and never lost a battle.

In 1753 he arrived home, happily married to his friend's sister, and at peace with the world. He was awarded a peerage, settled his father's debts, paid off the mortgages on the Styche estate and turned the squire into the country gentleman he was born to be! For his own family he purchased a property at Walcot near Shropshire's border with Wales, small but in delightful surroundings, and settled in England gladly. Twice he was recalled suddenly to India to settle urgent problems — one being the aftermath of the terrible episode known to history as the Black Hole of Calcutta. But he returned to his family to what seemed a bright future, when his old physical problems flared up again bringing pain which could be relieved only by drugs. Nevertheless he was involved in national affairs and elected MP for Shrewsbury to serve under William Pitt.

The House of Commons proved a more provoking battleground than the steamy jungles of India with bickering, rivalry, and jealousy over holders of office and their supporters. Clive came under attack for his spirited defence of Pitt. Political enemies spread innuendos against him and the fortune he had accumulated in India, with such venom that Clive was forced to take legal proceedings. His rewards from the Company he had saved, and from Indian potentates rescued in the interests of peace, were seriously at risk. Yes, maybe he *had* resorted to some subterfuge ... but conscience was clear because circumstances and lives depended upon it. Now his whole future was at stake.

The wrangle dragged on before he was vindicated but the stress affected his physical condition, and doctors advised a move to a drier spot. He located Oakly Park near Ludlow and Lady Clive turned it into a happy home. Robert enjoyed choosing and filling it with paintings, and was appointed Lord Lieutenant of the County. But sadly his health worsened with constant pain from gallstones despite increased opium doses. Depression overtook him as he struggled for more than a year with this and with repercussions from his legal battle.

Then suddenly, unexpectedly, his adventurous but troubled life came to a dramatic end. 'An overdose of opium unwittingly taken' ran the Press report next day and inferred that one dose too many — or too soon — in his condition could bring on a heart attack. Questions were asked, inevitably. Did he choose to die? He was 49 years old; his eldest son just 20 and the younger one only five years of age. And there were two daughters, with a loving, supportive wife. . . . Perhaps it was the mystery of his burial which accentuated the doubts, and that Lady Clive remained silent in her grief. Clive died at his London house in Berkeley Square (purchased to be near the Commons) and his body was taken secretly for burial in an undisclosed grave. Suicides were then buried in unconsecrated ground. The speculation was, perhaps, natural.

It was 100 years later when renovations to the flooring of the church at Moreton Saye revealed the truth. Below a slab in front of the chancel was Clive's lead coffin. And there it stayed while new parquet flooring was laid over it. Perhaps his death had to be mysterious. Everything in Robert Clive's life was unpredictable. No one seeing the schoolboy kicking his heels against the church steeple dreamed that he would play a major part in bringing to England that glittering Jewel in the Crown which played so large a part in our once great empire.

Voice Of The Stars

'**O**LD MOORE' must have been a determined fellow as a lad in Bridgnorth to have taught himself to read and write. He was born in 1657, on the 29th January, into a very poor home which had been partly hewn out of rock on the side of a hill, with only the frontage built of brick. A few of these quaint houses still stand in Bridgnorth, but the Moores' home has crumbled away.

It is unlikely that this boy had the slightest encouragement toward scholarship from his family. It was as much as they could do to eke a bare living. However, as soon as he could read, Francis (as he had been named) began delving into books on anatomy and medicine. By his mid twenties he had obtained a physician's licence and was recognised as 'Dr Moore'. But it is as 'Old Moore' that he has gone down into history, mainly through his later association in London with a medical man of somewhat doubtful repute named John Partridge. Moore became assistant to this shoemaker-turned-doctor, who was now enjoying association with high society as an astrologer and almanac maker.

Back in Shropshire the Bridgnorth man's association with an astrologer would have provoked wide curiosity. The county had always been noted for its fascination with superstitious cures, charms and divination, though it was the moon, rather than the stars, which had engaged their imagination and inspired respect, even to the point where girls ceremoniously revolved and curtseyed out of doors before the first new moon of the year. Seventy years earlier

Shakespeare's *Midsummer Night's Dream* had featured the popular superstition that the moon and human destinies were linked — 'A calendar, a calendar! Look in the almanac; find out moonshine'. But Charlotte Burne, the 19th century researcher into Shropshire folklore, quotes an intriguing German superstition: 'it is wicked to point at the stars because they are angels' eyes'.

However, in the middle of the 17th century when Francis Moore was born, astrology was being treated with some respect. Apparently when he joined John Partridge in London, they enjoyed some notoriety and the benefits of high society together.

Moore set up in business on his own account when he was 41, combining his roles of medical man and astrologer. He brought out his first almanac chiefly as an advertising ploy to popularise pills of his own concoction. It was published in 1699 under the title *Kalendarium Ecclesiasticum*. But he retained links with his birthplace and six months later came the issue of his more celebrated *Vox Stellarum* (the voice of the stars) which he dedicated to the Recorder of Bridgnorth who was also its MP, Sir Edward Acton.

Surprisingly, Francis Moore never became old, despite the later, more popular, title of his almanac. He died in 1715, at the age of 58, but his almanac was taken over by others and lives on after three centuries. In Moore's own day the predictions were mainly weather forecasts, but today its scope is wider, including football, angling and birthday guides, as well as recording achievements in the Olympic Games.

The Coalport Story

To produce beautiful wares which invoke the near reverence of experts centuries later involves combined skill, genius and enterprise. No one person can claim full credit. But among those responsible for creating and marketing Coalport China the name of John Rose deserves acclaim. He was a Shropshire boy who must have been one of Thomas Turner's first apprentices at the Royal Salopian China Manufactory at Caughley.

Turner himself had come up from Worcester in 1772 or thereabouts, bringing refinement to the pottery works established 20 years earlier in Shropshire's Severn valley. It was Squire Edward Brown of Caughley Hall who had realised the potential of the available resources of clay and coal lying on his estate alongside the river and begun to produce earthenware. Then came Turner with his knowledge of porcelain manufacture, and under him John Rose finished his apprenticeship in 1793. Within a short time the new canal, built on the opposite side of the Severn, lured John Rose and a partner to move across to Coalport and open a factory in a picturesque setting on the banks of the Severn. The river and canal, of course, provided easy adjacent transport. It was an historic decision.

In less than five years Rose was able to purchase the original works from his old bosses at Caughley. The combined operation developed and improved their products until the highly popular bone china emerged from the factories at Coalport.

But there was heartache, too, during those years for

John Rose and his partner, Edward Blakeway. Pioneering costs money, a great deal of money, and some financial investments proved less than sound. The trauma and heavy shadow of bankruptcy overtook the partners, but thankfully all was not lost. The works were purchased by financiers, and Rose remained in control of the firm which retained his name as John Rose and Company. It progressed so well that in 1814 another china firm, of which John Rose's brother was a partner, was absorbed into the business. Now Coalport was making its name as a major centre in the country for both practical and high quality decorative wares.

The name of John Rose was further enhanced when his researches enabled him to replace the injurious lead-based glaze with one based on felspar to overcome the dread of disease from 'potter's rot'. The Royal Society of Arts recognised this enormous contribution to the welfare of both industry and workers in 1820 by awarding a gold medal. The favourable publicity was welcome and a commemorative mark went on the wares forthwith. Further recognition followed in 1837 when Queen Victoria ascended the throne. Commissions were given for a quantity of hand-painted jugs portraying delicate floral sprays for the royal palaces, the initials VR traced in gold proudly displayed.

As with all caring entrepreneurs, John Rose opened the way for other achievers. Their signatures on original paintings won fame for ceramic artists. These included William Cook, who excelled in vivid panels of fruit and flowers on a turquoise base, and Thomas Dixon (also specialising in fruit and flowers) whose whole family came into the business as painters or to burnish the rich gilt decoration. John Randall was the most versatile of them all. After an impressive career in ceramics, famed for his studies of bird life, he took early retirement (at about 60) to pursue other talents. He acquired a post office at Madeley and combined it with printing and bookselling while developing his own authorship, painting with his pen graphic illustrations of industrial life in the Severn valley, drawing from his personal experience at Coalport. How wonderful for him that he could enjoy two satisfying careers by living to be 100 years old!

John Rose enjoyed nearly 50 years in management before his death in 1841, handing on a high reputation and a good working base to brother Thomas and a nephew, W. F. Rose, who were joined by William Pugh. The company went on to earn a medal and prizes at the Great Exhibition of 1851. The Queen commissioned a dessert service — her gift to Czar Nicholas I of Russia, richly decorated with ornate crests painted by William Cook. It created a sensation at the Crystal Palace, as did the Rose du Barry dessert service bought by Lord Ashburton. At the entertainment given there by the Queen, the Coalport commemorative plate, sporting the Royal Coat of Arms, was given a place of honour on the royal table.

A well known product enjoyed by more humble households the world over is the ware designed, it is claimed, by a Coalport artist to illustrate the legend of a mandarin's daughter and her forbidden lover fleeing from capture by changing into doves — the familiar, well loved blue Willow pattern.

As with all ventures, fortunes fluctuate with changing times, war and industrial unrest. Also, as river and canal transport was superseded by road and rail, the Severnside site was not so strategic, so Coalport china with its traditional patterns and lines took its workforce over the border into Staffordshire where it now continues production under the wing of the famous Wedgwood firm. Happily, a site at Coalport is established within the exciting museum complex there, which recounts the story of that great enterprise in the Severn valley.

Love And Marriage

T HE name of Hannah Phillips would have been long forgotten had it not been for the quaint custom featuring the Maidens' Garlands. In many areas of 18th century Shropshire, funeral tributes for a girl who died unwed included a specially made garland of rosettes and streamers, lovingly fashioned in crepe paper over a wooden frame shaped like a bell, from which a pair of white gloves would hang. It was designed to be placed on the coffin when carried into church or was sometimes borne in front of the procession by a young girl, giving an almost bridal touch to the sad occasion. Long after personal memories, and even her family had perished, the garlands remained, suspended over the pew where the late lamented maiden had been accustomed to sit. A tribute that she died in her virginal purity? Or a silent lament that she had not lived to fulfil her expected role as wife and mother.

Hannah Phillips was not the first girl to be thus mourned, but her name is always connected with the custom in Shropshire because her garland still survives in Astley Abbots parish church, as do seven others in Minsterley church, each carrying a date of birth and the girl's initials. Only in Hannah's case is the full name displayed, recording the date of death, 10th May 1707. Apparently hers was an especially tragic story — almost on a par with the famous ballad of the Mistletoe Bough. On the eve of her village wedding to a local lad, so anxious was Hannah to ensure that everything was perfect for the

morrow's event that she slipped over to Astley Abbots church to check over the final arrangements. All completed, she bade her well wishers farewell on that lovely summer night — and was never seen again! The story persists in local histories that on her way home the ill-fated bride slipped off the ford by which she crossed the river and fell into the water at the very spot where an underground cave lurked beneath the surface.

Her body, it is said, was never recovered. If this was so, the funeral garland must have been the only focal point at the mournful ceremony which usurped the wedding. Maybe this is why there are more details on her now faded and crumpled garland than on most of those sad relics.

For Mary Carter of Sibdon Castle near Aston-on-Clun a much happier custom was established. After proceeding from the castle for her marriage to Robert John Marston in 1786 she was delighted to find the arbor tree in the centre of the village decked with flags. She took it to be part of the village's celebration of her nuptials. But the date coincided with that of Oak Apple Day and tree dressing was already established to commemorate that important national event — the Restoration of the Monarchy, in which Shropshire had played a very special part because it was one of their own oak trees which successfully sheltered King Charles II after his defeat at Worcester.

It may have been a very happy coincidence that the tree was decked with flags on Mary Carter's wedding day at Clun, but she was so delighted that she left a legacy to perpetuate the festivities and the custom was established of giving a cutting from the tree to each new bride, assuring her that if the cutting took root it augured well for the fertility of the marriage! The decked arbor tree is still a prominent feature in the village.

Not unnaturally *finding* a husband occupied the thoughts of young girls in Shropshire, as elsewhere. Six Market Drayton girls followed the ritual of sitting up until midnight one Hallowe'en, each placing a shift to hang over the back of a chair in front of the fire. As midnight struck they repeated a charm which lasted for exactly ten minutes, and the girl whose shift moved was the one who would marry first. Presumably they then had to wait until 'Mr Right' came along for there was very little they could do to advance their own fortunes.

A much easier way of finding out one's future prospects was adopted by small girls at Clee St Margaret with the co-operation of that tiny harbinger of fortune, the lady cow or ladybird. Placed on the back of the hand, it was tossed away with the bidding:

'Lady cow, lady cow, fly away, flee!
Tell me which way my weddin's to be,
Up hill, or down hill, or towards the Brown Clee.'

But at Wenlock it appears that the locals relied upon hempseed, sown in a circle at midnight on some specially appointed day with the words 'Hempseed I sow. He that is my true love, come after me and mow.'

For a lovelorn bachelor the way was made rather more difficult. He had to find a five-barred gate and cut three notches in it and, moreover, to keep it up for nine nights in a row! Alternatively, he might walk around the local church at midnight three times and as he reached the porch thrust his sword through the key hole, saying 'Here is the sword, but where is the sheath?' It was promised that as he returned home he would meet the woman he was to marry. But could she have been up to any good, one wonders — to be out and about at such a time? It would be well beyond midnight by the time the would-be suitor had completed his perambulations. . . . Another Shropshire custom is thought to have a link with the old Bible story of Rachel and Leah. If a younger sister married before an older one, the elder sister must dance in stockinged feet at the wedding. Happily the Biblical precedent was not followed so far as to force the groom to take on both sisters. And if the elder sister's plight was judged to be a hardship, pity the elder unmarried brother of a bridegroom. He was required to dance in a pig trough!

Village marriage ceremonies seemed to be a signal for rejoicing for all the neighbourhood. Pretty floral and greenery arches were erected along the route to the church for the happy pair to walk beneath, decorated with streamers, paper heart replicas and bannerets with cordial messages. One Stoke-on-Tern bride in 1829 must have been a popular girl. She recalled the neighbours strewing the way before the couple with flowers, and draping each side of the gate with strips of white cloth on which silver spoons, tankards, watches and ornaments belonging to neighbouring farmers were fastened.

Sadly, not all marriages are made in Heaven, and from Saxon times until the middle of the 19th century the practice of wife selling was the alternative to divorce for the poorer folk, and seemed to be considered legal so long as certain rules were followed. These required it to be a public transaction, the woman being brought through the turnpike gate (in the days when these were enforced) and conducted to the market place with a rope halter around her neck. In some cases a document was prepared in advance asserting that both were party to the sale. In Shropshire the usual price was five shillings and a quart of ale. Apparently there was no shortage of buyers and a happy adventurer into matrimony seems to have been one John Aston of Strawbarn. He married four times and was heard to claim that his last purchase at Wenlock Fair in 1880 was his best bargain. For an outlay of 18 pence he triumphantly led home, still haltered around her neck by the former husband's rope, Bride Number Four to Coalbrookdale. Another old book records a bargain hunter purchasing two wives on the same day, and leading both home with the same ceremony as this was considered part of the legalising procedure.

But there were couples determined to preserve their marriages. When they bathed, each in turn in the same tub of water (it all had to be hauled out of the well then) it was customary for the second bather to spit in the water before entering. It may not sound very salubrious now, but spittle had real significance in the not far distant days. It was customary to spit on the hand before shaking it to clench a bargain. In 1883 Miss Georgina Jackson wrote of 'the singular fashion of greeting which prevails about Ruyton-of-the-Eleven-Towns (in north-west Salop) and probably in other parts of Shropshire. A man seizes his friend's hand, holds it flat open, spits on the palm, then wipes it with his own lower arm, beginning from the elbow, gives it a sound open-handed clap, and finishes off with a vigorous shake.' She goes on to say that farmers, butchers and countryfolk in North Shropshire spat on all money paid to them as otherwise it might vanish 'like fairy money'.

Returning to the bath spitting, it was supposed to prevent a quarrel between couples, according to Hannah Munby of Shifnal who was never one to flout ritual. Indeed, any effort designed to keep a marriage going was worth trying if only to prevent one's neighbours 'Riding the Stang' — a custom by which a quarrelling couple would be 'shown up'. Straw-stuffed effigies representing the couple would be hoisted on to long poles by a yelling crowd banging on tin pots and pans who halted outside the offending pair's home. The crowd would chant doggerel rhymes, shout accusations and consign the straw figures to a bonfire in front of the couple's windows!

The Miller's Daughter

THE lonely young man who arrived unheralded and unannounced in the village of Great Bolas in 1791 must have been something of a puzzle to local folk. He seemed uncommunicative about his purpose or plans, and the mystery deepened when, after a brief stay in lodgings at the farm of Miller Hoggins, he asked his host for a job at the mill and settled down for an indefinite stay in Bolas.

Weeks went by, and though the newcomer, who gave his name as Harry Jones, was civil enough, he gave away nothing about his past life, or said why he wanted to stay. In dress and manner of speech he was distanced from the other village men, and was new to the lifestyle of the miller's household. But before long his demeanour changed, the shadowed expression lifted from his eyes, and he moved around the village with new assurance. The reason was not hard to find. Sarah Hoggins, the miller's daughter, was a lovely girl — and quite obviously she had fallen in love with this mysterious stranger. What did it matter if he was so reticent about his affairs? He probably had a good reason. Here and now he was under daily observation by her family and nothing transpired which gave any cause for concern. The future was all that mattered. Sarah was prepared to stake hers upon her heart's prompting. It seems that the miller had no objection. Sarah was married to the lonely stranger and became Mrs Harry Jones.

But not for long. As suddenly and inexplicably as he had arrived in Bolas, Harry Jones departed — in response to a message, according to the miller. He returned, but went off again several times and rumour began to circulate in the village, for no one likes to be kept in the dark over interesting developments. Had there not always been something odd, something 'different' about him? 'Gentleman Harry', some of the lads had christened him. Why had he appeared among them so suddenly? What and where had he run away from? Speculation was rife. Thoughts of smugglers or of 'dandy' highway robbers (this was often a gentleman's crime) began floating through the minds of the more suspicious villagers. It would have been only human if Sarah herself had suffered misgivings.

Then came the day when Harry returned to take his wife for a holiday tour in the country, during which they passed Burleigh House near Stamford, Lincolnshire. They paused to look at it, and according to several reports of the scene the young husband asked his wife's opinion of it. 'Sarah was entranced', says Arthur Mee, who wrote with such feeling about 'The King's England', and the astonished girl was told that this was her new home. She was the Marchioness of Exeter! Her husband was really Henry Cecil, who had just inherited the property and the title of Earl of Exeter.

It was a day of revelations, though not all of them happy ones. It transpired that Henry's self-imposed exile from his family and former friends had been the result of grief through a broken marriage when his first wife absconded with (of all people) a curate! Divorce (and the death of the ex-wife) had followed while the sad young man found refuge in the peaceful village bounded by two rivers — the Tern and the Meese. It was a happy chance which brought him to the mill and the healing love of a simple, unaffected village girl. Within a short time, the Earl and Sarah went through a second marriage ceremony at St Mildred's in Bread Street, London, in the groom's real name, and took

46

their place at the ancestral home where the first Queen Elizabeth found refuge in her girlhood.

Sarah gave her husband an heir, and three other children were born to them. Theirs was truly a fairytale romance, and though neither parent was destined for a long life, it is pleasing to record that the mysterious stranger who fell in love 'on the rebound' was nevertheless true to that love when his circumstances dramatically changed.

Ritual, Rhyme
and Revels

'To everything there is a season', says the sage, and Shropshire has always been mindful of annual events, beginning of course with 'first footing' on New Year's Day. Not only do households prefer a dark haired male to be their first visitor, but in the north of the county first footers are required to parade right through the house, entering at one door and exiting at the other, being duly rewarded for their pains. On 2nd February Candlemas Day is linked with the appearance of the little garden 'first footer', the snowdrop, called by the charming name of 'Candlemas Bells' and bunches may be brought into the house to mark the occasion.

A more vigorous February celebration in Ludlow was the highly organised Shrove Tuesday tug-of-war, started off by the mayor dangling the tug rope (with a blue knob at one end and a red one at the other) from an upper window of the Market Hall. Two rival teams struggled for it by climbing on team members' shoulders and the tugging began in earnest. The red knob had to be pulled far enough to be dipped into the river Teme or the blue knob, via the Bull Ring, into the Corve to make a 'score' — and the whole process could be repeated until the winners were declared. How sad that it had to be discontinued around the mid 19th century because it evoked unmanageable strife!

Often such a boisterous day of merrymaking would include cock-fights and other dubious sports, but children at Ellesmere and Wellington in the north provided a genteel example by 'Clipping the Church', encircling it, hands linked, with backs to the building, then side-stepping around it.

Jacqueline Simpson tells a beguiling tale (albeit with tongue in cheek) in *Folklore of the Welsh Border*, featuring an old couple who wanted to use up some unleavened dough with their left-over Christmas pudding. Should they bake or boil it? They disagreed so violently that they smashed a stool, a broom and some eggs in the fracas! But the spirit of thrift prevailed. The broken furniture provided the fuel, the eggs glazed the crust — and the cake was christened by combining their two names, Simon and Nell! However unlikely the tale might be, it appears that to Shropshire goes the credit for inventing the now famous Simnel Cake — a rich fruit mixture, crusted with saffron and topped with almond icing — part of Mothering Sunday celebrations each March, beginning in the 17th century. This day gave respite to Lenten self-denial. A holiday was granted to all absent sons and daughters so they might return home, bringing a modest 'treat' for mother (sometimes Simnel cakes), to visit the mother church, scene of christenings and baptisms, then enjoy a special dinner together.

Palm Sunday (or the day before) was a signal for gathering substitute palm branches for church decoration to mark Christ's entry into Jerusalem. Picnic parties roamed Pontesford Hill for twigs of willow and to search for the lost Golden Arrow, said to have been dropped or buried by a long dead king, and finally to snatch a twig from a 'haunted' yew on the hilltop, dashing headlong downhill to dip a finger into the pool at its foot.

Good Friday found every worthy housewife baking buns which had to be marked with a cross — to keep away bad influences, according to superstition. Then Easter Day was celebrated in both Herefordshire and Shropshire by hardy souls who rose before dawn and climbed the nearest high hill to watch the sun rise as a symbol of Resurrection.

More boisterous proceedings would follow, for Shropshire is one of three counties where 'heaving' contributed to the festive programme of Merrie England until about 1888. On Easter Monday the men toured around the houses armed with a chair decked out with greenery and ribbons, with the intention of placing the women therein and heaving them above their heads (or extracting a forfeit in lieu). On the following day the roles were reversed, the women combining strength to hoist the men, who might well have been even more apprehensive. Victims were seated in the chair, raised from the ground three times, then twisted around! It appears that this custom's link with Easter, boisterous (and perhaps irrevent) though this seems, lies in its demonstration of the Resurrection.

Oak Apple Day was celebrated throughout the county with enthusiasm and a holiday demanded in song:

> 'Royal Oak Day, Royal Oak Day,
> The twenty-ninth of May,
> If you don't give us a holiday,
> We'll all run away!'

Maypoles were erected, the Queen of May elected, Morris dancers took the stage and everyone enjoyed the fun. Some opportunists disrespectfully renamed this 'Pinchbum Day' — indicating a certain penalty for spoilsports refusing to wear the traditional sprig of oak. This was justified, it was said, by its association with the King having to be pinched from time to time to keep him awake when searchers neared his perch in Boscobel's oak and danger increased. History is preserved in many ways!

Harvest time had its own long established programme, of hard work and long hours, culminating in a race between farms to finish first. However, before demolishing the last sheaf of standing corn a pause was made to observe the ceremony known in Shropshire as Cutting the Gander's Neck. The sheaf was divided and tied into four bunches, the upper section being the neck at which the reapers swung their sickles. To add excitement (and danger?) contestants were sometimes obliged to stand with their backs to the target! Harvesting was completed to the cheers of spectators. On then to the Harvest Homes with their variety of fare, depending probably on the fortunes of each farmer. Herefordshire and Shropshire folk fared much better than most on chicken, hares, hams, beef and bacon followed by tarts and puddings for the sweet-toothed.

Country customs die hard. In the lambing season a rather macabre version of tree dressing landed a Shropshire farmer in court in recent years. It appears he feared the old superstition that if the bodies of dead lambs were given normal burial on his land future lambing would be at risk. Lambs not yet born would not survive. So he adopted the old custom of lodging the pathetic little carcases in the forks of his trees. He was prosecuted. Witnesses testified in his defence, but sadly for him magistrates put hygiene before ritual. The farmer was convicted and fined!

Because death is no respecter of persons — or of seasons — the quaint custom of 'Telling the Bees' was observed at any time of the year, and probably still is. It seems there is something very special about these little creatures that can only communicate itself to the hooded keeper, upon whose management and economics depend the success of the honey harvest:

51

'A swarm in May is worth a load of hay,
A swarm in June is worth a silver spoon,
A swarm in July, not worth a fly.'

It certainly appears that the tiny heads conceal an alert brain. Shropshire folk supported the tradition that the death of a beekeeper must be quickly communicated to his hive or the little creatures would take umbrage and fly away or would themselves expire. There are several interpretations of the ritual — it must be done in the middle of the night, the hive must be tapped with a stick and told 'The master is dead' (or 'Your friend's gone'), and so on. But some insist that the right time is when the funeral leaves the house, when the coffin is lifted so must the hive be raised (in salute?). In North Shropshire the hives were included in the mourning ritual by tying crape to them.

There is a tradition that no one must use bad language near the beehive, which tends to support the findings of a bygone researcher that the bee has special status, is in touch with the 'hereafter', and its function is to prepare the way for the newly departed person! Apparently this idea stems from the little creature's association with Samson's riddle in the Book of Judges — 'Out of the strong came forth sweetness'. Honey produced in the carcase of a lion provided the key to the conundrum he put to the Philistines. Perhaps there is something in the assertion in 'Deutsche Mythology' that the bee's 'prudent way of life serves as a bright example to mankind' and that the bee 'must surely be a relic remaining from the Lost Paradise and the Golden Age.'

Can there be a higher compliment?

Beelzebub And
The Black Sheep

T HE strange thing about Humphrey Kynaston was that
      he won more respect as an outlaw than he did as a
member of the local gentry.

Humphrey was the spoiled youngest son of Sir Robert
Kynaston of Hordley, born in 1470 and seemingly
unwilling to grow up. When he reached 21 — possibly with
the idea of installing some sense of responsibility into him
— he was given the keeping of the family seat at Myddle
Castle near Nesscliffe, which lies between Shrewsbury and
Oswestry. Unfortunately it became a rendezvous for the
bad company he had kept since boyhood. The castle fell
into neglect and decay while debts mounted up. Then
came a brawl at Church Stretton, ending in murder and
flight from the scene.

From then on Humphrey was a hunted man, forced into
hiding, living from hand to mouth. But, surprisingly, he
made a name for himself, not only for his dexterity in
avoiding capture by the sheriff's men, but for sharing the
spoils of audacious robberies with the poor and needy.

As outlaw and highwayman, the erstwhile squire seems
to have combined the roles of Robin Hood and Dick
Turpin with marked success and popularity. So long as any
Nesscliffe villager had food in his larder, neither Kynaston
nor his horse went hungry, though their only home was a
cave cut into the face of the cliff which gave the village its

name. The interior of the cave was divided by a stone pillar, so master and steed had the luxury of separate apartments which, combined with the cave's arched entrance at the top of a flight of stone steps, evinced a faint echo of the former Kynaston grandeur!

Scamp though he was, Humphrey became a legend of which Shropshire is quite proud. He finds a place in all the local history books. It was the villagers who named his horse *Beelzebub*, and not without reason. To throw pursuers off his tracks he had the horseshoes fitted back to front, without apparently impeding the animal's marvellous prowess.

On one occasion Humphrey was lured into the courtyard of a local squire and offered ale from a silver cup. Even as he drank he realised his wily host had had the gates locked behind him. But he nonchalantly finished the drink, swiftly pocketed the cup and spurred *Beelzebub* to leap over his captors and sail above the locked gates to freedom. Small wonder the villagers thought the horse to be supernatural! Even so, it is stretching the imagination a little far to believe that *Beelzebub* once leapt from the top of Nesscliffe Hill and over to Ellesmere to escape pursuers. It is a distance of nine miles!

One feat which everybody seems agreed upon is that when Kynaston's escape was barred because Montford Bridge had been tampered with (planks removed by the sheriff's officers) the outlaw turned aside to the river bank and *Beelzebub* leapt 40 ft across the water! The place is still known as Kynaston's Leap — so it has to be true!

It is strange that of all the Kynastons, Humphrey is the best known one in Shropshire history. In 1516 he was pardoned, went to live peacefully on a modest property in Welshpool and presumably ended his days there. It is nice to read that the Kynaston family have preserved the pardon document which seems to indicate that, after all, there was some unexplained redeeming grace to be found in their family black sheep.

The Darby Dynasty

ABRAHAM Darby was 37 years old when he felt sufficiently secure in his ironworks business at Coalbrookdale to draw up plans for the building of his own house. The site overlooked the ironworks on the western side of the Dale. This was in the year 1715, and for three years past he had enjoyed the tenancy of Madeley Court, a Tudor mansion a mile and a half away. But now, thought Abraham, it was time to establish a permanent family home and, perhaps, to welcome more sons to join four year old Abraham Junior. As soon as the house was built he would develop an equally important ambition — the building of a Quaker meeting house to serve his own family and eight others living in the district, most of whom were employed at his ironworks. Abraham had worked hard to reach his position. He deserved success. He was at the prime of life and all seemed set fair.

Nine activity-packed years had elapsed since he came to settle in Coalbrookdale, where he had found the derelict ironworks ripe for redevelopment. The area neighboured on the Staffordshire of his boyhood where metalworking craftsmen would be in the market for top quality wrought iron rods to transform into chains, locks and tools.

And so it had proved. Abraham got the old ironworks going where others had failed because the coal they fed into the roaring furnaces had introduced impurities. His star was in the ascendancy when he proved coke could generate the right heat and content to produce quality wrought and cast iron — and the Shropshire clod coal lying at hand was ideal for turning into coke. Later his method was to revolutionise the iron industry nationwide and prove a key factor in the Industrial Revolution.

But before the new house was completed Abraham was stricken with a mortal illness. Even so, he partially achieved his dearest wishes by convening the first Coalbrookdale Quaker meeting in his nearly finished home early in 1717, and one can imagine his mixed emotions as he took his seat on that very special occasion.

Only 39 years old, and on the brink of his full potential, Abraham died on 5th May 1717, leaving his six year old son and namesake with only a tenuous hold on a small share of the business. While pursuing and diversifying his products the first Abraham had been obliged to take a partner. After his untimely death a mortgagee all but snatched away the Darby family's share of The Coalbrookdale Company. Happily a Quaker friend grasped the situation and secured the Darbys' investment.

By the time 17 year old Abraham II took his place in the business it was thriving. In addition to supplying the trade with iron, local fairs were now retailing kettles, cooking pots, frypans etc from the Darby foundries. Then came the dramatic advent of the steam engine, bringing a demand for cast iron pipes, wheels, rails and a host of other essentials. By the middle of the 18th century Coalbrookdale had become the hub of Britain's industrial life and the most important iron-making district in the world.

The second Abraham's specific achievement proved him a worthy successor. He adapted coke-fuelled furnaces to produce good bar iron from pig iron (so called because the refined metal seeped through beneath the furnace into sow-shaped moulds with channels branching off at right angles from the body, as if for feeding piglets!). So keen was Abraham II that he once spent six days and nights without a break at the furnaces until he perfected his system and was carried home asleep by a party of workmen. How he endured the marathon defies imagination, for a visitor once described the night scene at the roaring furnaces as 'a peep into hell'.

Now the Darbys could afford to celebrate success. Three hundred workpeople, as well as the poor of the district, were fed on a fat cow, ten large fruit puddings and two hogsheads of drink, spread on four tables under canopies in a meadow beside the river. The second Abraham fulfilled his father's dream and established the first Quaker meeting in Coalbrookdale — though he also failed to make old bones. He died at 51, leaving a reputation for business integrity and sincere piety.

The third Abraham was only eleven years old then, but the firm was well run until he and his brother Samuel, reached their teens. They expanded, taking over farmland to include horses, cattle, fruit and cereals in their disposable commodities by 1774. Then, under Abraham Darby III came the most exciting innovation of all, the building of the very first iron bridge. It was a major leap in British history. Abraham and Samuel were appointed builders with a group of important industrialists heavily involved. Based on the Shrewsbury architect's plan allowing for a 90 ft span, it was estimated to cost £3,200. But the erection of the iron pieces, when made and laid out on the river bank, quadrupled in cost to £12,700! It was an amazing project. There was no previous construction with which to compare and no one could possibly anticipate inevitable pitfalls and setbacks. But it rose ... strong, slender — and unique!

New Year's Day 1781 was a red letter day for Coalbrookdale — for Britain, even — when the bridge was opened to traffic. It drew worldwide crowds, many declaring it to be an additional 'wonder of the world'. It has been picturesquely described as 'the marriage of grace and power'. Engineers and construction experts came from all over the Continent, greatly impressed by the technological achievements of the whole district, which has been declared many times to be the birthplace of the Industrial Revolution.

It was fortunate that Abraham III's business acumen developed early in life because, like his grandfather (the founder of the firm), he died at the age of 39, and also left a son of the tender age of six years. This boy was named Francis. For the first time in the company's history there was no Abraham to succeed. Management fell into the hands of various cousins and in-laws for two decades and the business suffered something of a decline, due in part to prevailing circumstances in Britain. But in 1830 a fourth Abraham appeared to represent the new generation. With his brother Alfred he reversed the trend, dividing off some sections of the business between other branches of the family and initiating reforms to modernise that which he retained.

The brothers' foundry was judged to be the largest in the world by 1851 which, happily, coincided with the date of the Great Exhibition at the Crystal Palace. The fame of the Darbys rose again. Beautiful ornamental gates exhibited there were later installed at the entrance to Kensington Gardens, where they may still be seen and admired. The statue of Andromeda bound as a captive at the mercy of a sea monster, was purchased by Queen Victoria for £300. Thousands of visitors were entranced by the ornamental fountain holding aloft on its summit a chubby child riding a graceful swan.

This was, perhaps, the Darbys' own swan song. Risen in status, they took their place in society, leaving management to trusted employees. In 1925 the last of the Darbys took retirement, thus ending the enterprise of a remarkable family. Five generations of business integrity and Quaker influence had stamped indelibly the Darby image around the Coalbrookdale area.

In their wildest dreams the Darby forbears could scarcely have anticipated the renaissance that took place in the Severn Gorge. Today the iron bridge still attracts a host of visitors every year. The award-winning assemblage of museums and heritage displays make this one of the most rewarding and delightful of excursions.

The Adderley Pew Feud

KEEPING up with the Joneses is nothing new. But strangely, the bitter class warfare between the Needhams of Shavington and the Corbets of Adderley Hall raged within the hallowed precincts of Adderley parish church and was a very public affair indeed. No prudish inhibitions prevented them from washing their dirty linen in public, and from keeping the affair up through two generations.

It so happened that for many years in pre-Reformation days, the Needhams had been independent of a parish church, worshipping in their own chapel complete with resident priest at Shavington Hall, which suited them very well. But when Elizabethan legislation banned private chapels and took away their licences everyone was compelled to attend the parish church. The Needham family had no choice in the matter. There was no road to the church from their home, so they took advantage of a short cut through Adderley Park in order to join the vicar's flock at Adderley — and were consigned to the nave, even though Sir Robert Needham was lord of the manor.

He complained bitterly and long to both vicar and patron of the church, John Corbet, both of whom enjoyed the privilege of a family pew in the most prestigious spot, the chancel. He considered his family on equal terms. But it so happened that in the distant past the lordship of his manor had come under the jurisdiction of a long dead Corbet who had authority at that time to demand 40 days war service (in the event of need) in return for his patronage. This

61

requirement, even when commuted to a sum of money in lieu, had lapsed by the 15th century. But when the dispute arose between the two families in the early 1600s as to who should sit where in church, rank was pulled. Mr John Corbet demanded of Sir Robert payment of that old feudal obligation which had effectively established the Corbet superiority. Sir Robert refused to concur and Corbet promptly blocked the short cut through Adderley Park! As patron of the church he was prepared to do nothing in regard to the complaint over the pews.

Temporarily the vicar found a compromise. He was a bachelor at that time and invited the Needhams to use his family pew in the chancel, giving the Needhams and the Corbets equal status in church. It was an excellent solution until the vicar fell in love, got married and was obliged to reclaim his family pew. Complaints and arguments were fruitless. The Needhams were returned to the nave. But when Sir John Needham was created Viscount Kilmory in 1625 his situation was exacerbated. A pew in the nave was no place for a Viscount! Then John Corbet was honoured with a English baronetcy, whereas the Kilmory title was Irish and therefore inferior! Checkmate?

Fortunately in 1629 Lord Kilmory salvaged his dignity and independence by getting his private chapel at Shavington rebuilt, relicensed and reconsecrated, though Sir John intervened to ensure that the services permitted were on a limited scale. Burials could only be carried out at Adderley, for instance.

By 1632 both the Viscount and Lady Kilmory had died and one might expect the hatchet to be buried also. But no. Sir John Corbet scored a macabre victory in the following year when his footman died. He forced the vicar (a patron had such powers) to have the man buried alongside Lady Kilmory's resting place in the chancel! That lady's son, the second Viscount, rose to defend her dignity. By a persistent series of appeals he got the Earl Marshal of

England to issue a decree in 1634 which enforced the exhumation of the Corbet's footman and his reburial in a more modest but (one hopes) peaceful spot.

Flushed with success, the second Lord Kilmory went further, over the head of the church patron (still the same Sir John Corbet) and direct to the King for a licence to build on a chapel for his family in Adderley church. The Archbishop of Canterbury granted it, and a very fine place it was when erected in 1637, in a spot adjoining the chancel and lavishly decorated with the Needham heraldry. Now Lady Corbet entered the fray, obtained the key of the Kilmory chapel from the parish clerk and took a small army of servants with the family to occupy it. The contretemps went on for weeks. When ejected forcibly, the Corbet party returned with an armed guard in the churchyard for protection!

Unfortunately Lord Kilmory's outraged protest to the venerable Archbishop of Canterbury was sabotaged by the outbreak of the Civil War, in which Sir John Corbet fought with the Cromwellians. When the King was defeated and the Archbishop thrust into the Tower, Lord Kilmory was defenceless. And to add insult to injury he was fined by the new government! Sir John Corbet must have been a very satisfied man indeed when he returned to Adderley after the war.

The Day Of
The Packman

Fᴿᴏᴍ village to remote village he plodded, alongside his patient, burden-bearing horse, over highways that were so rough, and in winter so mud-soaked, that man and beast were obliged to skirt along the edge and find footholds on the scrawny turf which fringed the track. On the more frequented roads between villages, where the coaches of the gentry were obliged to pass, a firmer passage composed of quarry stones and boulders gave a more stable surface, but so rough was it that a traveller in 1770 despaired of his safety and complained of having to hire men to support his chaise and prevent it from overturning. In those conditions the packman with his solitary beast was better off picking his way on foot. The entrepreneur with a wheeled vehicle or a string of laden horses confined his activities to the village and town fairs.

It was a brave man who set up in business as packman or pedlar to catch the custom of countryfolk. Just such a one was William Cantlin, who included the rugged, isolated moorland of the Clun Forest in his 'patch' in the last decade of the 17th century.

At that time, before the advent of the village shop, the villagers' only alternative was to make the excursion to the nearest town or the periodic fairs. Those journeys could be fraught with danger, so the travelling salesman made a valuable contribution to rural life. Though he might appear only two or three times during the year, his role extended far beyond the selling of merchandise. He was newscaster and postman rolled into one. His welcome was assured. The enterprising traveller would develop into a good teller of tales. Scandal, crime, Parliamentary problems, skirmishes on the Continent and discoveries from farther afield all made for impressive discourse.

From somewhere in his bulging pack the visitor would produce copies of new songs, handbills about entertainers, pictures of Society belles and cheaply printed advertisements of the latest fashions. These would inspire village maidens to attempt home-spun versions of the same, aided of course by ribbons, buttons, lace and other fripperies from among the haberdashery stock. Spurred on then by new confidence, his cutomers would avail themselves of his services as scribe — to pen love letters to lads in nearby villages and carry them on along with other messages or letters along his route. And, of course, there was always the more mundane stock in trade — pots, pans, tin kettles, earthenware mugs, jugs and other utensils as well as the basic aids to cuisine to supplement and improve the cottagers' diet, such as it was.

It was rare for the packman not to show up at the appointed time whatever the conditions or his own situation. But, sadly, he was only mortal and one day William Cantlin collapsed as he neared the Welsh border. Death claimed him before he could reach the next village. What was especially pitiable was that no next of kin could be traced and some doubt arose as to which parish should assume responsibility for his burial. Eventually it was the men of Bettws y Crwyn who undertook the sad task. They bore away the body along the high, bleak hilltop to the graveyard around their 500 year old church. Here the packman was laid to rest on a spot which commands a view over nearly all Shropshire, including the rough paths and lanes along which he had picked his way for so long. Seemingly his tale was told.

Nearly 200 years later there was a surprising sequel. The implementation of the Clun Forest Enclosure Act in 1875 required evidence as to the acreage to which the community was entitled. The villagers' acceptance of responsibility for the packman's burial 184 years before was recognised as proving their right to include the territory on which he died as part of their possessions. Thereby Bettws gained several hundred extra acres. A memorial stone was erected at the spot and inscribed 'W.C. descd here. Buried 1691 at Bettws'. Later the MP for Ludlow, Beriah Botfield, who was a botanist and a compiler of good books, recognised the significance of the story even into the 19th century and erected a carved stone cross, six ft high, to stand beside the original Cantlin stone. It has since sunk into a shapeless mound with barely discernible inscription, but is fenced off in its remote spot and some there are who will take the trouble to find it.

In death William Cantlin, humble pedlar, had unknowingly left an appreciable legacy to the village customers he had served so well in life.

Botany And The Bombshell

PERHAPS Charles Darwin became accustomed to pursuing his own inclinations regardless of consequences when he was still a boy living in the big Georgian-style red brick house called 'The Mount' just outside Shrewsbury. In 1809 he was the fifth child to be born into the local doctor's family (all within five years) and it was a sad day for them all when Mrs Darwin died soon after the birth of her sixth. Charles was then eight years old and was receiving some elementary teaching at home from his eldest sister. After a year at a day school in Shrewsbury he became a boarder in 1818 at the grammar school, a mile from home.

At the time the headmaster was Dr Samuel Butler, a distinguished scholar and disciplinarian. Yet he, though backed by Charles's stern, austere father, failed to arouse the boy from his customary lethargy and disinterest. He learned very little in school and lived mainly for the holidays when he could potter about outdoors. Unfortunately the father of the family was not of a temperament to make up to the children for the loss of their mother. Inevitably, though perhaps unintentionally, the moment he joined them in the home, he produced an atmosphere of tension. Since he was a huge fellow, six ft five inches in height and with a 24 stone bulk, it would be difficult to ignore his strictures and displeasure when his own high standards were not reached.

But the young family, and Charles in particular, were compensated somewhat by the warm affection and welcome received at Maer Hall in nearby Staffordshire, the family home of their mother, Susannah. She had been the eldest and favourite child of the famous potter, Josiah Wedgwood. Charles's early pursuits, fishing for tiny creatures in a quarry pool, tirelessly collecting coins and minerals, and outdoor sports, were much more pleasurable in company with the Wedgwood cousins as he grew into his teens, and were his only real interests. So much so that when Charles was only about 16 years old his father abruptly terminated his grammar school education. 'You care for nothing', he berated the boy, 'but shooting, dogs and rat-catching.' He ended his tirade by prophesying that his son would be a disgrace to the family. Oddly enough, Charles later claimed to have a life-long veneration for him, testifying to his father's kindness and wisdom!

In the long summer vacation after leaving grammar school, Charles attempted to smooth down his headmaster's scathing report on his low achievements by accompanying his father in pony and trap on his medical rounds. Bowling along in the Shropshire countryside, he was delighted to observe all the movements of bird life and scampering wild creatures in field and hedgerow. He loved riding with the Wedgwood cousins — probably with Emma in particular, for she was destined to become the one love of his life. Natural history was weaving its spell around him also at that time, and the collection of pebbles and beetles drew his searching eye. He relates one occasion when he captured two interesting beetle specimens, one in each hand, only to espy another scampering away. Popping one beetle between his pursed lips, he freed a hand to grab the third one in flight and was rewarded with a mouthful of

69

obnoxious fluid as beetle No. Two fought back from capture.

Despite Charles's poor showing at the grammar school, Dr Darwin sent him to Edinburgh to study medicine. Charles found anatomy lectures not only dull, but disgusting, and the only two operations he ever witnessed (in pre-chloroform days) quite horrifying. After two unproductive years, the doctor switched him to Cambridge University to aim for a degree and qualify for the priesthood. Charles enjoyed his three years at Cambridge, developing musical and artistic tastes, and an interest in natural science which drew him to the attention of the young Professor J. S. Henslow, a keen botanist. This led to an introduction to Adam Sedgwick, professor of geology. But Charles left Cambridge in the summer of 1851 with a low scholastic rating and no clear vocation for the ministry or anything else. So he planned a carefree summer, to begin with a geological tour with Adam Sedgwick and later to join the Wedgwoods for the start of the partridge shooting season. Tomorrow could take care of itself!

And so it did. Before reaching Maer Hall Charles had a surprise letter which changed his whole life. Professor Henslow had recommended him for a vacancy as a young naturalist on a voyage of discovery aboard HMS *Beagle*. A surveying expedition was to round the coast of South America, cross to the South Sea Islands and sail on to the Indian Archipelago, departing in one month's time!

Nobody had ever shown confidence in him before, and Charles wanted to leap at the chance to turn his outdoor pursuits into a possible career. But would his father agree? The post was prestigious but unpaid. With beating heart he faced the doctor that evening. Exactly as anticipated, he met a brick wall of resistance. The doctor assumed (and unkindly pointed out) that many others must have refused before the post was offered to Charles! It was a wild scheme. There must be something wrong with the project or the ship if nobody else had taken it. It would be useless and unsettle Charles for the priesthood or anything else. Finally came a challenge 'If you can find any man of commonsense who advises you to go, I will give my consent.'

Dejected and mortified Charles wrote to Henslow turning the job down on the grounds of his father's refusal — and left for Maer Hall to console himself with the partridge shooting. The Wedgwoods were astonished that Charles had missed such a chance. Uncle Josiah, a man of commonsense if ever there was one, urged Charles to retract his refusal before it was too late — and the doctor capitulated. Within a month the attractive, slender, blue-eyed young man was on board the *Beagle* committed to a three year expedition.

In fact, the voyage was extended and Charles was lost to Shropshire for all of five years. The *Beagle* encircled the world before returning on the 2nd October 1836, on what would go down into the annals of history as one of England's most famous voyages. The doctor was astonished at the change in his son. The indolent, pleasure-loving young man who dabbled with beetles and rocks had returned mature, purposeful, with a channel for his energies. His fame spread and for two years he wrote and lectured to an eager public about the voyage and his discoveries.

Then came a homesickness for Shrewsbury and Maer Hall and particularly for Emma Wedgwood — attractive, shapely, of medium height, with candid grey eyes and an abundance of golden brown hair. She proved to be the ideal wife for Charles, calm and reassuring in manner, well educated, musical and a delightful companion. His need of her was to be greater than he realised, for almost immediately he succumbed to a mysterious malady which stayed with him for life, though never satisfactorily diagnosed. It drove him to seek the warmer, drier air of

Kent and at Down House he and Emma spent the next 40 turbulent years. Here their ten children spent a happy childhood, Charles proving to be a fond, indulgent father.

Emma created a loving, relaxed home life, based probably on her own ideal childhood at Maer Hall. She bore with Charles's strange illness (some thought it imagined) and resolutely stood by him in the storm that broke when his controversial books were published. In 1859 *The Origin of Species* startled many. But not until *The Descent of Man* followed, did the word 'evolution' occur, revealing that his theory related to development of human life as well as of plants and animals.

Charles had waited 20 years before publishing, knowing his theory's conflict with Biblical teaching would cause an uproar in the Christian Church, and pain and disquiet among the families back in Shropshire and at Maer Hall, as it had done to patient, loyal Emma who commented sadly he 'seemed to be putting God further and further off'. The second book was not at first well received except by a few like-minded scientists and writers. Charles was lampooned and ridiculed in magazines, posters and the national as well as religious press.

Nevertheless the evolution theory spread throughout the world and gained wide acceptance. It brought Charles Darwin great fame, yet he suffered bouts of depression and inner conflict in his closing years. He died at the age of 73 of a heart attack in his garden. There must have been mixed emotions in the solemn burial in Westminster Abbey.

Shropshire's own memorial to the man described as 'Shrewsbury's greatest son' is the splendid statue erected in a premier position outside his old grammar school, which is now the public library. It testifies to the amazing acclaim of the pupil whose final school report almost drove his father to despair of him.

The Face In The Firelight

HANNAH Cullwick was born at Shifnal in May 1833, with so unpromising a background that no one could have imagined her as the centre of a secret romantic drama which would eventually mystify and astonish Victorian society. She was one of five children of a local saddler and the family was so poor that their mother would have thought herself in Utopia if she could have mustered eight shillings for weekly housekeeping. According to Hannah's later account she would sometimes be hard put to find three shillings to feed seven mouths!

By the time she was eight years old, Hannah had left Shifnal's charity school and was doing housework for a local woman before progressing to scullery work at the Red Lion Hotel. There market days were heydays, for she was allowed to wait on the farmers at dinner and received tips of one or even two pennies when carrying round the 'collection plate' after the final course. The generous donors got a respectful curtsy. Their tips augmented the family income until, all too soon, both parents died and the youngsters were left to pit their wits and energies against the daily grind to sustain themselves as best they might.

As housemaid to Lady Boughey of Aqualate Hall, Newport, Hannah discovered the great gulf existing between Upstairs and Downstairs. Alongside the benefit

of 'getting her feet under somebody else's table' she experienced the tyranny of insecurity — the threat of instant dismissal and homelessness for a trivial offence.

It was in the service of Lady Louisa Cotes, who was the daughter of the Earl of Liverpool, that 17 year old Hannah found an ally in Emma, the kitchenmaid. Her new employer owned the two country houses of Woodcote and Pitchford Hall, and while taking a temporary respite below stairs one tea-time Hannah fancied she saw, outlined in the glowing embers of the kitchen fire, a manly face made attractive by a well trimmed moustache. Emma, summoned to share the vision, acquiesced and predicted that this was a face which one of them would encounter one day. Fanciful? Wishing thinking, perhaps?

But so it proved, according to Hannah's later handwritten account. Four years later Lady Louisa was on a visit to London, taking Hannah along with her. Returning to Grosvenor Street after an errand, Hannah met a well dressed gentleman who spoke to her courteously before passing by. Though she did not recognise it instantly this, to use her own words, was the 'face that i'd seen in the fire'. Events were to prove this a significant meeting. Some would go so far as to call it a rendezvous with fate.

The gentleman turned out to be 25 year old Arthur J. Munby, a well-born man who was a lover of the arts and no mean poet himself. He was acquainted with many well known writers and painters, the celebrated pre-Raphaelites among them, and on terms of iife-long friendship with R. D. Blackmore of *Lorna Doone* fame. By profession Munby was a barrister but was never seriously attracted to the law, preferring to devote time to teaching (unpaid) at the working men's college and to freelance journalism.

What made him exceptional, for a man of his good

background and tastes, was an intense fascination with the working classes and with working women in particular. Though there was a degree of condescension and of philanthropy in this, there is no doubt that contact with the lowliest and even degraded types gave him some emotional satisfaction. He was fascinated by the rough skin, brawny arms, weatherbeaten faces and marks of drudgery. He seemed to see in rough, manual labour and lowly demeanour some kind of virtue that was uplifting. However, in his brief encounter with Hannah Cullwick in that London street he was also attracted to the combination of the usual badges of servitude (the striped print dress, apron and mob cap) with an unusual grace and bearing for one of her station. So momentous was the meeting and its consequences that 50 years later Munby's description of it was highly revealing and gives a graphic picture of Hannah:

'For, on the 26th of May, 1854, she was brought to me, a surprise of all surprises, by Him who brought Eve to Adam. A country girl, she was, a scullion at the Squire's. . . . A tall erect creature, with a firm step and noble bearing: her face had the features and expression of a high born lady, though the complexion was rosy and rustic, & the blue eyes innocent and childlike. . . . A robust, hardworking peasant lass with the marks of labour and servitude upon her everywhere; yet endowed with a grace and beauty, an obvious intelligence, that would have become a lady of the highest. Such a combination I had dreamt of and sought for; but I have never seen it, save in her.'

Munby took the trouble to trace the girl before she left London with her mistress, and it is obvious that he corresponded with her during the next ten years, though there are no clear records of the developing romance until Hannah found a 'place' in London, by which time Munby was renting the first floor of No 6 Fig Tree Court, Inner Temple. Within a few months he commenced the diary which was eventually to be his chief claim to fame.

References to Hannah show that while holding down her employment, she yet found time to attend the working women's college and to further her education with Munby himself. He delighted in her growing good taste in literature. She, in her turn, spent her meagre hours off in working in his home, finding her greatest pleasure in performing menial tasks for him as a way of demonstrating her growing love and her recognition of his class superiority over hers. This was always to feature very prominently in their relationship and it seems Hannah derived some strange pleasure in emphasising it, rather than taking the opportunity to 'better herself', which made their courtship and eventual marriage most unusual — and possibly unique. For a long time this made her the perfect foil for Munby's own eccentricity and absorption in studying the lower classes in their grimy and humble state.

Munby and Hannah met from time to time in London as he sought to introduce her to good music and other 'improving' arts but it was 17 years after their first meeting before he ventured to take her into his own service as maid of all work. Their love was a total secret between them, even when Hannah rubbed shoulders with neighbours at Fig Tree Court while prominently performing domestic chores for Munby and his two sub-tenants. For a time Hannah 'lived out', but eventually took to the truckle bed in the kitchen, and it was a further year before Munby decided he must 'do Hannah justice' after the long courtship and marry her. Strangely, Hannah was reluctant. It seems that she feared it would in some way destroy the mystique of their secret bond.

However on the 14th January 1873 in Clerkenwell parish church the knot was tied! Hannah was now 39 years old and Munby 44. Only a sonnet of Munby's exists to describe that strange day:

'How well I recollect our Wedding Day!
She did her black work with a beating heart;
Then wash'd herself and own'd a servant's part,
Waiting on me, and then she went away
Down to the kitchen bedroom where she lay
Among the pots, alone and quite apart;
There doff'd her servile dress, and with meek art
For once did make herself a little gay:
Her long dark cloak; a red stuff gown quite new;
Her black straw bonnet with white cap: Oh no,
No gloves, no flowers! "Massa, shall I do?"
She cries; "I have no looking glass, you know!
Now I am off! And mind you, all my life
I shall be servant still to you, as well as wife." '

And so it proved. The marriage made little difference to their master/servant routine, which produced a farcical situation whenever Munby entertained guests, particularly his own relatives. Despite his misgivings at the deception (which seemed to produce in Hannah a measure of hilarity) Munby went along with it as he could not bring himself to disclose the truth to his conventional family. But Hannah's scruples were now satisfied. She could live openly at Fig Tree Court, albeit in her familiar servant's garb. Now she slept 'above stairs' most of the time, though the marriage relationship seems to have had little of passion in it. Meanwhile her husband maintained his work among the poor and was often out enjoying life as a gentleman of good taste among convivial company.

But the scene changed when Munby persuaded Hannah to take a holiday with him. It appears that 'Mrs Munby' acquitted herself well on the Continent and even better when introducing him to her native county in the year following the marriage. They walked through Wellington to the small farm of Hannah's Cousin Gosling to spend the night in a cosy bedroom overlooking meadows golden with buttercups. They spent a couple of days with her brother, a Wombridge carpenter, where Munby seemed quite at home. He, it seems, could adapt better to a contrasting society than could his wife in her turn.

On their next visit to Shropshire they stayed at a Wellington Hotel with Hannah 'drest and adorned as a lady', enthuses Munby in his diary's record. Then they visited Church Stretton and climbed the Long Mynd before going on to stay at The Feathers in Ludlow and go shopping in Goodrich. Munby was delighted with Hannah's prowess, but on her return his wife cast aside all her finery with decided relief and made it clear that she was determined to keep to her own lifestyle and homely Shropshire dialect whatever her 'Massa' decreed. (That name for him was the slave-style corruption of 'Master'.)

In the summer of 1877, three and a half years after the marriage ceremony, it seems that Munby tired of the deception. After his parents' deaths his own fear of embarrassment was reduced. But Hannah was not co-operative, and after reaching something of a stalemate Munby decided to take a Continental holiday with his friend William Ralston, the Russian scholar. Hannah was despatched to her brother in Shropshire, under doctor's orders, though the malady remains unclear.

Munby then obtained a country home in Surrey, having benefited from his father's estate, and resolved to make a new start. Meanwhile, Hannah was energetically engaged in slapping wet fish into newspaper wrappings at her brother's stall in Oakengates Market, apparently recovered but still resolved to remain the simple country woman which was all she wanted to be. Her weeks in Shropshire had confirmed it. Two visits from Munby in that first year of separation failed to move her. He therefore moved into his new home, Wheeler's Farm at Pyrford, and found domestics to manage a bachelor domain. Now almost 50 years of age, Munby settled to the writing and book reviews which would occupy him for his remaining 30 years, while Hannah pursued her very different course. She accepted an allowance from her husband, but continued happily to help her brother and from time to time to take domestic jobs in other households when so inclined.

Munby and Hannah corresponded on affectionate terms; she did not appear resentful. She was capable of good English. She used the word 'factotum' in an appropriate setting in the same letter in which she wrote spontaneously in homely fashion. 'I love you more deeply nor ever you can think . . . how happy I am wi thinking about thee! How different to the common sort o'lovers — and how true thee bist. . . .'

It was a red letter day for Hannah, no doubt, when her husband returned to Shropshire to establish her in a cottage at Hadley after nearly a decade of indecision, and of only occasional meetings. He now created for her a home which he could share with her at intervals. His visits settled into something like a routine, despite one alarming incident in 1888 when a group of local pit boys accosted him. From his height, apparel and general appearance they suspected him of being the hunted Whitechapel criminal, Jack the Ripper! Fortunately a more trusting older pitman gave him shelter in a cottage until the coast was clear for him to continue his return to the waiting Hannah.

Over the next 13 years, Munby joined Hannah in her modest cottage home at fairly regular intervals and something of the old warmth flooded back during this compromise. The couple were more relaxed than at any time in their strange marriage, being now without need for subterfuge or pretence.

At Christmas 1902 they spent ten weeks together at

Hadley. Hannah then decided to return to Shifnal, her birthplace, for her remaining years. Here she found a tiny semi-detached cottage near the Red Lion inn where she had worked as a child and within sound of the church bells which had roused her to a life of labour when she was no more than eight years old. Munby visited her here for the last time in September 1908, for he was nearing 80 and weakening physically. Gazing into the glowing coals of her own hearth, with the beloved face at her side now, Hannah became reflective about their past. 'If all that was wrote in a play, and acted, folks'd say it couldn't be true!' she said.

Their long, tangled love story came to an end a few months later when Hannah died and was buried in the churchyard at Shifnal. Her husband's death followed six months later at his country home at Pyrford where he was buried. Not until his will was read to his astonished family did the Munbys learn of the unique romance of their 'bachelor uncle' and the national press gave wide coverage. 'Romance Revealed In Barrister's Will' was probably the least sensational headline of them all.

Munby's own words were dignified and well chosen: '. . . And whereas Hannah Cullwick servant born at Shifnall in the county of Salop and bred at the Charity School of Aston Brook by Shifnall has for forty five years and upwards been beloved by me with a pure and honourable love and not otherwise and she the said Hannah has during all that time been as faithful and loving to me as ever woman was to man. . . .' By his own decree Munby's graphic diaries, letters and other records were sealed for 30 years. But the rich documentation of Victorian life and personalities, interwoven with the story of this compelling love, was eventually edited with great skill by Derek Hudson in 1972 and published by John Murray of London. To this author and his publisher we are greatly indebted for preserving the account of Shropshire's strangest love story.

The Shropshire Lass

WHEN Prime Minister Stanley Baldwin left Downing Street to spend Christmas at his beloved Worcestershire home near Bewdley, he looked forward to nothing better than relaxing hours before a glowing log fire with a good book. It was probably in 1927 that he chose *Precious Bane* by Mary Webb for his Christmas 'treat' and the heavy burdens of state rolled from his broad shoulders as he was transported by the Shropshire novelist into the countryside she loved so much and depicted so beautifully.

Mary spent her childhood at The Grange near Much Wenlock and was taught by her much loved father to enjoy to the full the rural scenes around her, with all their intriguing tales, legends and customs. George Meredith was a teacher of private pupils and was more free to pursue these shared joys than most parents could have done, so the bond was close, especially after Mary returned from boarding school to run the home for her sick mother. During these years she got to know many of the local folk, absorbing their dialect and their native wisdom.

Twice the family moved house, first to Stanton-on-the-Hine Heath and then to Meole Brace, both places being very near to Shrewsbury so Mary's knowledge of the county widened. But sadly, by the time she was in her early twenties she developed the malady known as Grave's Disease from which she was never to escape, and when her father died in 1909, his daughter was devastated. The one bright spot in this dark period was Mary's friendship with the younger children's governess, a Miss Lory. She had been with the family for several years and had taken a great interest in Mary's early attempts at writing. Now this friendship, together with her love of good books, became Mary's greatest solace and she found an outlet for her feelings in writing — mainly, at that time, in verse.

Three years after the death of her father, Mary, now 31 years old, married Henry Webb, a Cambridge graduate who was then teaching at Weston-super-Mare. But Mary missed her native county so badly that the couple returned and rented a cottage in Pontesbury. Here Mary supplemented the family purse by growing and selling garden produce. She rented a stall in Shrewsbury Market. But she also began to develop her writing talents in earnest and in 1916 her first novel, *The Golden Arrow*, was published. It was the beginning of an all too short but delightful series in which the Shropshire countryside and characters were so graphically portrayed that for hundreds of eager readers Mary's beloved county was 'put on the map'.

The Webbs' move to Pontesbury brought them closer to the Shropshire hills known as the Stiperstones, around which many a legend has been woven and where, it is said, 'time stands still'. So perhaps it was natural for Mary to set her stories in bygone years peopled with simple hearted but superstitious village folk who were dominated by strong, forceful characters. Some of these claimed supernatural powers to back their authority. This became very evident in Mary's fifth novel, published in 1924 and which many claim to be her best. This was *Precious Bane*. It won the Femina Vie Heureuse prize, and it so impressed Stanley Baldwin that he enthused over it at a literary dinner and thereby brought it the acclaim which it deserved.

What was so appealing about *Precious Bane* was its skilful introduction of old customs and its delicate portrayal of the heroine, Pru Sarn, who was afflicted by a disfiguring cleft palate. Did Mary's own ailment (which produced a noticeable goitre in her throat) aid this sympathetic touch? She had been very sensitive about it in her youth. Setting the tale in an earlier period enabled the writer to bring in the old superstitions which stimatized a sufferer by associating the victim with evil. Thus, true to form, most of the villagers of that day ostracised the girl, who becomes a household and farm drudge.

In this book, too, the macabre custom of finding a sin eater to take on himself the guilt of one newly dead is cleverly woven in. Farmer Sarn had died suddenly, voicing terrible oaths and obviously unshriven. At the funeral his son Gideon creates a crisis by refusing to summon a suitable 'scapegoat' — a stranger from the hills. Across the coffin he himself demands the bread and cider (poor man's wine) which he solemnly imbibes as he intones the old chant:

'I give ease and rest to thee now, dear man.
Come not down the lanes nor in our meadows.
And for thy peace I pawn my own soul. Amen.'

Then they all throw rosemary into the grave in relief and are able to join at the end of the funeral feast in the 'holy song' called for by parson and sexton:

'With a turf all at your head, dear man,
And another at your feet,
Your good deeds and your bad ones all
Before the Lord shall meet.'

Other fascinating characters emerge — Beguildy the wizard, with Jancy his feckless but pretty daughter, but none is more welcome than the journeyman weaver who comes at the appointed season to gather up the yarn from each villager's spinning wheel and turn it into cloth for the

84

winter. He is handsome and dignified, turning all hearts.
But the story climaxes beautifully when he arrives one
morning to save Pru from being victimised by a dipping in
the village pond via the dreaded ducking stool. She was
being made the scapegoat by superstitious villagers
because 'bad luck' had overtaken the village.

But (in fiction at least) all is well that ends well. The
weaver's chivalry turns to love and Pru finds her deserved
happiness. In the final sequence the significance of Mary
Webb's intriguing title is revealed. Fingering her scarred
upper lip and summoning an old-time word to describe the
malformation which has seemingly turned into a blessing
by drawing her weaver husband to her, she names it 'the
bane . . . the precious bane'.

It is sad to record that Mary Webb did not live to
complete another novel, though there are many beautiful
poems and essays showing an amazing perception of detail
when describing the countryside, plant life and furred and
feathered creatures around her. She was writing her sixth
novel *Armour Wherein He Trusted* when she died in 1927
while visiting her old friend Miss Lory, succumbing to the
disease which had plagued her all her adult life. She was in
her mid forties and though the loss to Shropshire was
considerable, it is true that her twelve year writing career
left an indelible mark on the county and that recognition of
her genius came largely as a result of the generous acclaim
of the Prime Minister who lived in an adjoining county.

It is sad that she did not live to enjoy her fame to the full.
She was very conscious of her own mortality when she
wrote:

'The birds will sing when I am gone
To stranger-folk with stranger-ways.
Without a break they'll whistle on
In close and flowery orchard deeps,
Where once I loved them, nights and days,
And never reck of one that weeps.

85

'The bud that slept within the bark
When I was there will break her bars —
A small green flame from out the dark —
And round into a world and spread
Beneath the silver dews and stars
Nor miss my bent, attentive head.'

She knew that Shropshire life must go on without her.
But certainly she made it the richer for all lovers of the
county and of good literature.

The Voice In
The Wilderness

ELIZA Gardner must have been in her very early teens when she fell in love with the Shropshire medical student Henry Hickman. Unknowingly she hitched her wagon to a star, though it was to be a long time before his brilliance was fully disclosed. She corresponded with him while he was studying medicine in Edinburgh and had no means of knowing then that his lively mind would take him far beyond his intended role as a country physician.

Both young people came from farming families, Eliza being a Worcestershire girl whose parents must have been well established and successful. Their home at Leigh Court, near Worcester, was a country seat which had royal connections, having once been owned by Queen Elizabeth's favourite, the Earl of Essex. Henry had probably come of a more modest background, if a family with 13 children may be so described. He was the seventh child to join the household at the farmhouse in the hamlet of Lady Halton, and a few days later, in January 1800, was baptised at nearby Bromfield. Had he opened his eyes at the font in that medieval church he would have found himself gazing up at a canopy of brightly coloured clouds, ribbon-scrolled texts and angelic figures. The church possesses a quite exceptional ceiling of painted plaster.

The boy must have determined at an early age to study medicine for he was up at Edinburgh by the time he was 19, and was a Member of the Royal College of Surgeons by spring of the following year. Four months later he located premises in Corve Street, Ludlow, to commence his career as a doctor. Moreover, he now had a home to offer his Worcestershire bride-to-be and the Gardner family gave consent for their 17 year old only daughter to be wed in her Worcestershire village in mid-summer of 1821. Eliza's signature on the marriage document (it can be seen in the Worcester Record Office) is clear and positive. It must have been a delightful event in the village, and the young couple set off for Ludlow and their new life together in high hopes.

Though the next few years brought to the Hickmans four children to be supported, and produced a change of scene from Ludlow to Shifnal, the young doctor was able to devote every Tuesday of each week, between the hours of ten o'clock and four o'clock, to provide free medical care to the poor and needy. In so doing he sacrificed not only income, but also gave precious time which he could otherwise have spent on a study which fascinated him beyond all else, and which became the most urgent and important work of his life. This was the need — the desperate need — for some means of anaesthetising patients undergoing surgery. It was a subject which was being neglected by almost all the medical profession, despite the appalling trauma of operating on a fully conscious patient — an experience which distressed surgeons and patients alike. Some surgeons have left on record their terrible dread of facing the next day's work in the operating theatre — and yet very few had the vision to try and do something about it.

It seems that in the very year of Dr Hickman's birth, Sir Humphry Davy had suggested that a possible solution for deadening pain under surgery might lie in the use of nitrous oxide gas — yet no medical authority had followed up the scientist's proposition. Twenty years later, whether influenced by Davy's suggestion or not, young Dr Hickman became convinced that carbon dioxide could provide the blessed palliative. Night after night he came out of his laboratory to share with his young wife his exciting discoveries, and his sense of urgency that the attention of the Royal College of Surgeons must be summoned. Painstakingly he wrote details of such experiments as his limited resources allowed, and in 1824 published them at his own expense in a pamphlet which he entitled *A Letter on Suspended Animation.*

Finally he despaired of moving medical authorities in London and set out for Paris, leaving his family in the care of his parents-in-law in Worcestershire. Since this must have meant selling up practice and home, it was in every sense of the word accommodating of the Gardners. They, at least, must have been impressed by the young man's urgent desire to minimise suffering and danger from the surgeon's knife, and recognised that he was seeking no advantage for himself. When Hickman reached Paris he begged the French Academy of Medicine to study his documentation for the sake of suffering humanity everywhere. The French King is said to have sanctioned the appointment of a commission to study the matter. But nothing came of it, even in the country which was deemed to be the most progressive in the world in medical matters. The precious documents gathered dust.

It must have been a heartbroken husband and father who returned to his family empty handed after two years absence. Now there was nothing for it but to return to medical practice, and the Hickmans found a suitable house and surgery at Tenbury Wells. This place was nearer to Eliza's parents than the former surgery. And what a boon that must have proved, for it seems that the cause which had driven the young doctor for ten years past had indeed become a consuming passion. Within two years, at the age of only 30, the young man who would gladly have saved thousands from the agony of unrelieved pain lost his own battle for life and was carried back to Bromfield for burial.

Eliza, widowed at 26, had to maintain her children (all under the age of nine) by opening her Tenbury home as a school. What her feelings must have been at the apparent failure of her husband's life work can only be faintly conjectured. She could scarcely have been blamed if she had felt some bitterness, which may be why, 15 years later, she apparently made no response to a leading doctor who wrote to ask if she had kept her husband's papers.

Even so, she must have taken some comfort when belated recollection of the young doctor's work began to surface in France two years later. Some Americans had come forward with claims for pioneering painless surgery. An official at the French Royal Academy remembered the visit of the impassioned young physician from Shropshire in England. Following this came a letter to *The Lancet* naming Henry Hickman as the real pioneer.

Public recognition came on the 100th anniversary of Hickman's death. Many members of the Royal College of Surgeons attended a memorial service to witness the setting of a stone plaque in the wall giving appropriate dates, and ending:

'This tablet is placed here at the initiative of the Royal Society of Medicine, as a Centenary tribute to the earliest known pioneer of anaesthesia by inhalation. "Honour a physician with the honour due to him." '

The voice that cried in the wilderness had been heard at last.

Salopian Olympics

MUCH Wenlock has a unique link with the sporting world. It was their own Doctor William Penny Brookes who set the wheels in motion for the founding of the present day Olympics which began in Athens in 1896. Long before that, however, he aroused enthusiasm for competing in his own 'back yard' and though his main purpose was for physical welfare, he knew that to get the project off the ground there must be enjoyment, too. The first Wenlock 'Olympian Games' in October 1850 was great fun and very 'olde worlde' in style, with blindfold wheelbarrow races, pig chasing and an old ladies' race with a pound of tea for a prize!

In another 20 years the programme had become more sophisticated (more's the pity, perhaps?). By 1870 track and field events included quoits, high jumps and weight throwing. But tilting while clad in medieval costume, with the competitor aiming his spear to go through a ring which had been suspended over the course, must have been the 'special event'. It was Dr Brookes who launched the Wenlock Games each year with a rousing speech from the steps of the Gaskell Arms Hotel, after which began the parade of the athletes through the streets of Much Wenlock. Small wonder that by then around 5,000 spectators made the journey there. 'Brummies', Londoners and competitors and supporters from other towns and cities carried details of the contests back home until similar sporting events sprang up elsewhere.

Dr Brookes enthusiastically supported the spread of the

games countrywide by founding a National Olympian Association. He later contacted the organisers of the Greek Olympian Games which were being held in Athens, donating a small prize, and seeking support for an 'International Olympican Festival' at a future date centred in the Greek capital. King George of Greece responded to these overtures by presenting Dr Brookes with a silver trophy which was handed to him at the National Association Olympics in Shrewsbury in 1877.

Correspondence continued between Wenlock and Athens, and a French nobleman with similar ambitions came over to attend the Much Wenlock Games in 1890. He was invited to join the procession with the doctor. As usual, the whole town closed down its business and watched entranced the pennyfarthings, jugglers, tilters, Indian club manipulators and flower girls who enlivened the parade of athletes through the narrow streets. At the conclusion of the events, olive crowns were bestowed upon winners and medals issued. That great day saw another step forward in the revival of the International Olympics as we know them today with their multi-million pound worldwide backing.

Dr Brookes was at the heart of the Wenlock Games for more than 40 years during which other areas in Shropshire followed suit in varying degrees. Shrewsbury had a famous show on the Monday following Corpus Christi. It began with a parade of trade guilds led by the Mayor and Corporation with banners and emblems held aloft by the performers in medieval costume, many of them as recognisable historical figures. All wended their way to a venue at Kingsland for feasting, sports and games of which 'Running the Shoemakers' Race' was a firm favourite. A rough track was provided by cutting a mile long stretch of turf in zig-zag patches, at the end of which the competitor was confronted with a circle designed to look like a giant's face into which the runner was required to jump, landing squarely — if possible — on the giant's eyes. Great fun for those who could stay the course!

It was during the 19th century also that the Royal Shrewsbury School Hunt began. The school captain, called the Huntsman, had to dress in a pink jersey and stockings, wearing a velvet cap adorned with a crossed whips design. A Senior and a Junior Whip were equipped with whips and pink caps, while rank and file seniors called Gentlemen of the Run wore blue caps. Any other participants were designated as Hounds and the resulting cross-country runs must have been made more purposeful by the costumery and the hunter/quarry sport. These pupils also had the benefit of outdoor exercise on the Fives Court — a rectangular plot 71 ft long and 32 ft wide, enclosed on three sides by thick walls having a cement coating, and with a narrower base shaped something like a goal area at the far end. It was a bat and ball game played as singles or doubles. The school's early form of football called 'douling' (akin to rugby) was played until 1880.

For the humble poor, of course, more simple pastimes sufficed. An old fellow giving a paper at the Caradoc and Severn Valley Field Club in 1941 recalled his childhood of 70 years before: 'When I was a schoolboy in the early 'seventies we used to play at tip-cat, dogger, murky, bandy, prison bars, spiking the spinning-top — games one rarely if ever sees now. Even the marble games are different. We had iron taws, skimmers and tinkers which, when shied at the "puds" or "cogs" would sometimes knock the whole lot down. And we would erect catsgallows for leaping, with hazel sticks. Girls' games — skipping, tut-ball and five-stones — are perhaps still played. . . .'

Games of pursuit and capture are always exciting, and the old Shropshire favourite Prisoners' Bars is a more sophisticated form of 'tag'. It really needs a good sized play area where two rows of contestants stand in line to face each other, each side having a 'prison' base about 25 yards to their right, between the two rows where they will house their 'captives'. The game begins by the leaders tossing a coin. The losing captain sends out a 'chivy' (a decoy) to the centre ground between teams. One of the opposing team is sent out to catch him, tag him, send him to his side's prison base and return to his line triumphant.

The losing side sends out another chivy who takes his place in the centre, calls out 'chivy' and tries to escape back to his 'touchline' or even to his side's prison to evade capture. If he succeeds his pursuer would become chivy, and so on. If a team wishes to rescue one of their number from prison a team mate must run from home base to the prisoner, and claim him without being caught himself. This energetic game can go on until all of one side are captured. Or, if a time limit be imposed, the winners are those with the most prisoners.

A well known rhyme commemorates a riverside pastime that was more of a hoax than a game to be played . . .

'The finest pastime that is under the sun
Is Whipping the Cat at Albrighton.'

A stranger was told that local cats were strong enough to haul him across the river. A rope was attached to the stranger and its other end taken to tie to a cat on the opposite bank. The leader would then pretend to whip the cat, and at a signal his cronies would pull the rope and jerk the stranger into the water. Hopefully he could swim!

It is fitting that a county so closely connected with athletics should have produced a world famous swimmer in the person of Captain Matthew Webb, born at Dawley in 1848, who learned to swim in the river Severn. While quite a small boy he saved a brother from drowning there, and later rescued a seaman in the Mersey. Until his time swimming had been discouraged as a sport because of its discomforts and dangers, but in 1869 the Amateur

Swimming Association established it as a national sport.

Webb later served in the Merchant Navy and while still a junior officer he jumped over the side in a heavy sea to rescue another seaman, for which he was awarded the Royal Humane Society medal. He gained his title when given charge of a small vessel sailing from Liverpool and his name came to the fore when swimming the 20 miles between Blackwall Pier and Gravesend. But it was on 24th August 1875 that real fame came to him as the first man to swim the English Channel. He crossed from Dover to Calais in less than 22 hours.

Enduring long spells in the water, and his skill as a diver, held onlookers enthralled time and again until the tragic day in 1883 when, despite urgent warnings, the 35 year old swimmer plunged into the waters below the Niagara Falls for a small wager. He held the watching crowd spellbound for ten minutes, then threw up his arms and disappeared from sight! It was several days before his body was located seven miles downstream. Alas for rash courage — but of course Dawley is proud of him and a bronze portrait is exhibited to perpetuate his memory.

The Hebers Of Hodnet

'God bless the squire and his relations,
and keep us in our proper stations!'

I F all squires and parsons had been cast in the same
mould as the Heber family the passing of the
'squirearchy' might be something to regret. They showed
that the role of the Big House could be benevolent,
establishing a community spirit and a sense of 'belonging'
among villagers.

This was the atmosphere in Hodnet, near Market
Drayton, around the year 1800 when Richard Heber was a
boy, rubbing shoulders with village families before going
up to Oxford University. He was 31 when he succeeded to
the family estates, and his 21 year old brother, Reginald,
was at Oxford winning an impressive reputation for
scholarship. Their only sister Mary completed the Heber
trio, and each of these three was to contribute in entirely
differing ways to the village history.

When the younger brother graduated from University it
transpired that he had a vocation — to follow their father
into the Church. He was not yet old enough to take Holy
Orders so he set off on a two year journey into Russia and
Eastern Europe to widen his horizons before getting
married and settling down in Hodnet as rector. His
brother, the squire, gladly appointed him to the living, and
with his young wife he settled into the old rectory. Then
Richard left village affairs in his capable hands and set off
to enjoy some overseas travel himself.

97

Hodnet may not have been the most adventurous scene for an outstanding young man with a lively spirit, but Reginald Heber proved to be a delightful, caring parson with a concern for all parishioners, whether of his own flock or of the dissenters. He found time also to develop his talent for verse and hymnwriting. One of his best loved (still much used) compositions is *Holy, Holy, Holy, Lord God Almighty*. The second famous one, though out of fashion now, is the missionary challenge which inspired a response from many eager young candidates in the second half of the 19th century. It was probably first heard at Hodnet, but well into the 20th century schoolchildren all over Britain were singing in morning assembly:

'From Greenland's icy mountains,
From India's coral strand;
Where Afric's sunny fountains
Roll down their golden sand;
From many an ancient river,
From many a palmy plain,
They call us to deliver
Their land from error's chain.'

The sentiments expressed were exactly suited to the climate of the times — those heady days of patriotic pride and unquestioning confidence in England's ability to benefit the world, and its vast empire in particular. In Reginald Heber's soul was an uninhibited faith in the Christian gospel and in his country. The rector's fame as a hymnwriter spread far beyond Hodnet and was to last for more than a hundred years.

Meanwhile the squire was happily following his own bent. At Oxford he had acquired a knowledge of the Greek and Latin classics, and in 1815 on his first trip abroad he commenced what turned out to be the ruling passion of his life — gathering together a vast and valuable collection of books. Returning to Hodnet Hall he built a library and filled both this and a London residence with literary treasures. When he successfully contested the seat for the representation of the University in 1821 he added a library at Oxford, and eventually did the same in Brussels, Ghent, Antwerp and some other locations. Small wonder that he remained a bachelor. All he asked of life was freedom to buy and to browse.

Life was good for all the Hebers and for their village in this setting. But, after 15 years of parochial ministry, life for the younger brother took a new turn, transporting him far beyond Shropshire, even though he had recently planned and built a comfortable new rectory at his own expense. In 1823 he faced up to his own missionary challenge and sailed for India as Bishop of Calcutta.

The Hebers' sister Mary now entered the arena. She had married Rev Charles Cholmondeley, who stepped into the new rectory to serve Hodnet with the same fatherly concern as his predecessor. His wife was a most capable partner, familiar with all the village families since childhood. Meanwhile the squire was contentedly absorbed in his growing collection of books which he acquired in threes — one copy to read, one to loan to friends and the third to keep in stock! His became one of the largest collections in England. He also became founder member of the celebrated Athenaeum Club in London. It was a typical scene of English village life.

Then came a bombshell from India. Reginald Heber, after three years serving a diocese greater in extent than Europe with brilliant success, lost his life in a tragic accident just before his 43rd birthday. The whole village united in mourning his loss as they awaited the return of the bereaved family.

It was only five years after this that Rev Charles Cholmondeley died, so by 1831 the squire's sister was a widow with four young sons. But she was a resourceful woman and when the squire himself died, leaving her the Heber estate for her lifetime (to revert afterwards to the Bishop's family) she rose to the occasion with resolution. By then the financial affairs at the Hall were in a parlous state. Richard Heber had lost sight of all prudence in pursuit of those splendid volumes. There was nothing for it but to resolutely dispose of the library to finance the restoration of the estate. Mary tackled the situation superbly, proving to be the capable administrator of the family, and, withal, a force to be reckoned with.

She has been described with amusing, yet affectionate candour in the autobiography of her granddaughter and namesake Mary Cholmondeley, *Under One Roof*. When the railway came to the area she did not allow her natural disapproval of the noisy, smelly innovation to deprive her of the benefit of fast travel. She reported to the railway station for her first journey and demanded that her own carriage be hoisted on to a truck so that she should not travel in a public compartment seated opposite to 'a person with whom she was not acquainted'.

As usual she got her own way, proceeding aloft in style, in her own carriage with her four sons somehow seated around her dressed, her granddaughter surmised, in the blue coats and long white duck trousers which she habitually chose for them. Moreover she resolutely refused to pay a fare. Why should she pay for a seat which she had declined to occupy? Never once did the ticket collector succeed in extracting so much as a penny out of her. Hopefully the notoriety of having a passenger travel in such style was sufficient recompense. The spectacle must have been unique.

When Mary's own life drew to a close, her departure from the village scene was entirely in keeping with her lifestyle. She lay in state at Hodnet Hall and villagers processed, two by two, round the candle-lit coffin. It was the last time that old custom was observed. With Mary

Heber a way of life had also departed. She was cast in a distinctive mould.

The Hodnet estate passed, as directed in the late squire's will, to Bishop Heber's eldest daughter, whose husband added that distinguished name to his own. Today their descendants, Mr and the Hon Mrs A. Heber Percy, throw open the beautiful gardens of Hodnet Hall to the public from April to September each year.

Talk Of The Devil

I T would be comforting to think human resources could outwit the Devil. No doubt this accounts for the popularity of old legends featuring His Satanic Majesty as a lumbering giant approaching with evil intent and being repelled. One tale tells of him having a grudge against the Mayor of Shrewsbury, and proposing to wreak vengeance by damming up the river Severn at some strategic point to drown the town. With this in mind he set out (from Wales) with a spadeful of earth, but lost his way. Lumbering along the Wellington road he was met by an old cobbler returning from Shrewsbury with a sackful of boots and shoes to repair.

The story was put into rhyme by an anonymous Salopian many years ago and appeared in the magazine *Shreds and Patches*. It begins:

> 'Now this cobbler was famous the country around
> As the very best hand that was anywhere found
> At the mending of shoes that were getting unsound;
> And every fortnight or so he went around
> And collected the shoes that folks could not use
> And the boots that required repair,
> And he got a good heap, for his charges were cheap
> And of business he had a large share. . . .'

As the tale unfolds it reveals the astute mind of the cobbler who, on learning the evil purpose of the giant, rose nobly to the defence of his customers. 'How far is it to

Shrewsbury?' asks the now weary giant, to which the cobbler replies 'You will never get there today, nor even tomorrow — look at the boots and shoes I've worn out since I started back from there!' Thus discouraged, the weary foe is said to have dropped his lump of earth on the spot where now stands the Wrekin. And alongside the hill, where he scraped his boots before retreating, stands the Little Ercall.

The village of Worfield, just north of Bridgnorth, has a tale of the Devil's interference in human affairs which also involves stone moving. It was planned, the tale goes, to build a church on the highest point. But the Devil objected and every night he removed the stones which had been laid during the day and workmen found them next morning on a lower site. Tired of trying to overcome this, the workmen eventually gave in and accepted the new site. It may even have turned out to the worshippers' advantage! Arthur Mee gives such a lovely description of it 'set in quiet watermeadows, with old gabled houses . . . by a wooded hill' and mentions 'a gem of 14th century glass' gleaming still in a south aisle window, that the siting seems to have brought no evil consequences whatever.

It seems incredible that a man should take on a gamble with the Devil, but it is claimed that a former owner of Ightfield way up in the north of the county once took him on and won! Moreover the Devil was made to pay a forfeit — to plant an avenue of trees leading to the church. What a very praiseworthy means of repayment for a gambler to choose. The tale goes on that the Devil swore to exact a revenge when the gambler died, whether buried within the sacred walls of that church or in the graveyard, so once again we hear of the compromise commonly adopted under such threat — that the departed one should lie neither inside nor out. The tomb of the gambler (of the name of Mainwaring) was placed in the wall of the church.

Gambling with the Devil is one thing, but to dance with

him seems the height of folly. Nevertheless the four stones known as the Devil's Rocks, rising like pillars at Dawnton Castle near Ludlow, are said to be four women who did just that and suffered the consequences. Many a medieval preacher must have used them in sermonizing, for it is not always easy to command the attention of a congregation. A parson at Bomere warned his flock of dire consequences for failing to attend divine services and it is said that one Christmas Eve when few heeded the summons, the village was swallowed up by flooding and is only faintly discernible at intervals in the depths of Bomere Pool.

But, further west, it is probably in the long, hump-backed hill formation known as the Stiperstones where the Devil's influence is said to be felt most. On the summit five projecting rocks stand against the skyline like the humps of some prehistoric monster. Charlotte Burne, a painstaking researcher in the second half of the 19th century, met an old countryman who claimed that the rock formation on the hilltop occurred when the Devil was coming from Ireland with his leather apron full of stones. Climbing the Stiperstone hills exhausted him. He sat to rest on the top and when he rose again his apron string broke and the stones were scattered. 'In hot weather', the taleteller added, 'if you go up there you may smell the brimstone still!'

Mary Webb was familiar with this terrain and in her enthralling novel *The Gold Arrow*, she describes it as 'a mass of quartzite blackened and hardened by uncountable ages . . . the scattered rocks, the ragged holly brakes on the lower slopes were like small carved lions beside the black marble steps of a stupendous throne.' And the 'throne' on the hill crest? It is a rock formation which can be seen on a clear day as being shaped like a huge armchair which has just been vacated. The superstition grew in years gone by that this was indeed the Devil's Chair and when concealed from sight of watchers below by grey mist or sleet he had

105

taken his place, screened himself from sight and attracted huge rolling thunderbolts to make his presence felt. It was a sign to dwellers in the plain and lower slopes to get their livestock under cover and hurry for shelter to their scattered homes. The Devil's Chair, says Mary Webb, remained inviolable, taciturn, evil . . . no one cared to cross the range near it after dark.

A reassuring addition to this tale was told by the lead miners who worked in the hillside of the Stiperstones, though it has to be admitted this was related more than a hundred years ago to Charlotte Burne. 'Of all the countries in the world the Devil hates England most because we are good Protestants and read the Bible. Now if ever the Stiperstones sink into the earth, England will be ruined. The Devil knows this very well so he goes, whenever he can, and sits in his chair on the top of the hill in hopes that his weight will flatten it down and thrust it back into the earth, but he hasn't managed it yet and it is to be hoped he never will!'

Regrettably it would seem that the Devil has been very busy in Shropshire in times past, for in addition to the best known Devil's Chair there is also the Devil's Mouth on the Church Stretton to Ratlinghope road and the Devil's Dingle near the Wrekin. Hopefully the tales which relate his defeats are not so far fetched as they first seem. After all, the Book the Devil loves to hate says, quite unequivocably, 'Resist the Devil and he will flee from you!'

Penmanship and Puritans

DESPITE its legendary introspection with the Devil and all his angels — or perhaps because of it — Shropshire produced an astonishing number of religious writers.

This may well have been due to encouragement they received by having access to the premises in Market Square of the Wellington publishers Houlston & Son. They were also printers and booksellers, thus providing a ready market for their publications and Houlston's became the main evangelical publishers in England. Successful women writers included Mrs Mary Sherwood who came to live in Bridgnorth in 1795, Hesba Stretton (real name Sarah Smith) who was born in Wellington, and Mrs Humphrey Ward who was educated at Shifnal boarding school. All three wrote with evangelical emphasis in the early 19th century, yet were highly popular and influential even a hundred years later in Britain. Miss Stretton was a co-founder of the NSPCC and her best known children's book *Jessica's First Prayer* so impressed the Czar of Russia that he ordered it to be included in the curriculum of all Russian schools. Contemporary male talent in that period of evangelical enthusiasm was represented by Bishop Heber, Patrick Bronte (then a curate in Wellington) and Patrick Anstice, mainly as hymnwriters and poets.

It is true that none of these quite measure up to the stature of the author, preacher and one time chaplain,

Richard Baxter — perhaps because it was not their destiny to meet the traumatic challenges which faced the Puritan in the mid 1600s.

Richard Baxter was born at the home of his grandparents in Rowton, near High Ercall, in 1605 and here spent his childhood until joining his parents in their black-and-white house in the village of Eaton Constantine. His later fame and attainments are the more surprising because his educators consisted of a strange sequence of unprincipled and unqualified tutors. Then a brief period of good schooling at Donnington was followed by another poor offering under the tutelage of yet another incompetent teacher at Ludlow Castle, instead of going to university as he hoped. His highest achievement there is said to have been his skill with playing cards under the instruction of the Clerk of the Kitchen!

However, the influence of his father's sincere piety and that of a group in Shrewsbury, brought him to a state of grace and understanding in spiritual matters. He joined the Anglican ministry and moved to Bridgnorth in 1640 as assistant to the priest in charge of St Leonard's church. Later events were to ensure that the little house in which he lived has become a landmark, and bears his name on the wall beneath the eaves of the dormer window.

His stay there was quite brief and within a few years the course of his life was overrun by the traumatic demands of the Civil War. His conscience impelled him to throw in his lot with Parliament and the early days of the conflict found him at Wem, helping to prepare that town's defences against the Royalists. But his role was as chaplain and throughout the war he moved from place to place as his duties required. What were his feelings, one wonders, as he watched the Parliamentary forces burn down the church where he had ministered and the castle where he had studied, together with other targets for destruction at Bridgnorth?

After hostilities ceased Baxter moved just over the county border to Kidderminster, hoping to settle to parochial life and the writing career which had so far been denied him by swift moving events in the country. But he was sorely grieved at the administration under Parliamentary rule — Cromwell's dictatorship and the traumatic days leading up to the execution of the King, to which he was totally opposed.

Unfortunately, however, it was the Restoration of the Monarchy and his writing career which in later life brought him into personal danger and trouble with the law. His *Paraphrase of the New Testament* was declared to be libellous, injurious to the authority of the Church and consequently undermining the State. Brought before the notorious Judge Jeffreys and charged with seditious libel, he defended himself with courage and dignity. Jeffreys was a fellow Salopian with the title Baron of Wem, but had no feeling whatever for the prisoner at his mercy. 'Thou art one of the greatest rascals in the Kingdom,' Jeffreys harangued him and would obviously have liked to penalise the old nonconformist by a far greater sentence than the 18 months imprisonment handed out.

Though then 80 years old, Richard Baxter survived the rigours imposed and lived on for another six years, leaving behind him a number of devotional books, a reputation for fearlessly following his own conscience, a host of influential friends and a far greater respect for nonconformity. Among his books *The Saint's Everlasting Rest* is probably the most notable, but his autobiography came out five years after his death under the title *Reliquiae Baxterianae*.

It was an honourable end to an outstanding career. Judge Jeffreys had died two years earlier — in the Tower of London!

Caradoc's Last Stand

ALTHOUGH centuries have rolled by since Caradoc defied the Romans, his name is far from forgotten. All over the Midlands are sites named after him, scenes of his prowess at one stage or another in his nine year struggle against the Roman invaders. When reading of the tremendous odds against him, it is easy to see why he stands out as a truly heroic figure, and no less than three neighbouring Midland counties compete in claiming that theirs was the high hill from which he made that last epic stand.

It would seem, on balance, that the rugged slopes of Shropshire's Breidden Hills, bordering on Montgomery, provide the most likely spot, and that all other areas named Caradoc, or Caer Caradoc (including those in Herefordshire and Worcestershire), mark stages where the Britons fought rearguard actions as they were thrust relentlessly north and westward. Fifty thousand well equipped Roman troops had been despatched by the Emperor Claudius to tame the island which had eluded the clutches of the Roman Empire for a hundred years. The historian J. Edward Parrott, MA LLD, claims that Roman soldiers were so intimidated by the knowledge of past failures and by the celebrated prowess of the Britons' leader, that they had mutinied on the way. But sadly (for Caradoc) the mutiny was put down, the Romans landed unopposed and swept inland and westward until that last stand.

So came the day of reckoning. The Britons were

marshalled behind a rampart of stone breastworks raised
near the summit of the hillside. Down below, at the foot,
flowed a wide river forming a barrier which the Romans
must cross before ascending to meet the onslaught of the
defenders. While the Romans paused at the brink, their
commander Ostorius Scapula went forward to weigh up
the situation and perhaps test the depth of the waters.
Caradoc snatched the opportunity to step forward and
rally his troops, willing them to make this last stand against
the implacable weapons of the skilful, well disciplined
Roman army.

He made an imposing figure, kingly, soldierly, a blue
cloak flung over his shoulder. From his helmet sprang the
customary horns, his bronze shield was carved in spiral
metalwork of Celtic design, his sword hilt and shoes were
inlaid with blue enamel — and he was an impassioned
speaker. Small wonder that his troops were devoted to him.
He was a born leader but all historians agree that jealous
tribal chiefs in the county failed to rally to his support at the
crucial time.

Though his men fought valiantly, hurling a storm of
missiles down the hillside as the enemy forded the river
and scrambled upwards, the Romans linked their shields to
form a wall of defence and broke through the stone
breastworks by sheer weight of numbers and weaponry.
Once behind the defenders' lines, auxiliaries emerged
from among the legionaries and charged upon the now
retreating Britons, who were slaughtered in huge
numbers.

Then came the great betrayal. Caradoc escaped capture
and fled for refuge to the court of his stepmother,
Cartismandua, only to be basely betrayed by her into the
hands of the now triumphant Romans. How could she?
Why did she? We shall never know. Was she tired of the
continuing struggle against Rome, and preferred to
receive the cultural benefits offered by Roman occupation?

111

Whatever the reason it has gone down as one of the shameful betrayals of history, and Caradoc, with his wife, child and brother, was carried off in chains to Rome. Paraded through the streets as the greatest prize in the Roman General's triumphal procession, he saw for himself the famed luxuries and architectural treasures, and must have wondered why Rome should covet possession of Britons' poor homes and territory.

But, to some extent, the whole tragedy was redeemed when he was brought before Claudius, and this scene has been handed down to posterity! Caradoc presented himself with dignity and spoke with quiet courage which so impressed the Emperor that he and all his family were freed from slavery. An unnamed writer has left us with his interpretation of that famous address:

'Emperor greetings! It had been more mete
Were I now come to pledge alliance
Than to plead for my life. I am unworthy of't
No more than thou, hadst thou my friendship sought.
I was a prince whose hand ruled many realms.
My line, from where it sprung within the mists
Of generations, bears me for a pace
And passes on into unmeasured time.
— Enough! I saw the purple hills of Severn,
And there beheld the heel of Rome.
— Far to the west, beneath the sunset, lies
An island, girt by ocean. There ye shall see
Green hills from willow'd banks rise gently forth
Where running waters in the sunshine sleep,
Cloth'd in deep shade. There ye shall see wide plains,
Ridg'd with their grey-green slopes, and far beyond
The blue of shadow'd mountains. — I fell,
And now plead life from thee, oblivion
My death, my life thy monument of grace.'

Echoes From
The Trenches

WILFRED Owen, destined to become one of England's greatest war poets, was 21 years old and working as a tutor in France when the Great War broke out. He would have been keenly aware that for the third time in his life his future hung in the balance. His tutoring appointment was the first job in which he had really succeeded since leaving Shrewsbury Technical School five years earlier, but as the war gathered momentum it became inevitable that he must return to England to seek whatever new role presented itself. Nothing in his life until now had remotely suggested the Armed Forces.

He had been born in 1893 at the home of his mother's parents, the large house in Weston Lane, Oswestry, known as Plas Wilmot. For four years he had known the warm security of family life there while his mother ran the household for them all and his railway clerk father provided for his family as well as looking after the sizeable property and gardens. But a dramatic change occurred on the death of the grandparents, whose wayward son had depleted their dwindling finances before disappearing abroad. Plas Wilmot with its familiar, homely contents had to be sold by public auction, debts paid, and what remained shared between Susan Owen and her two sisters. Tom Owen took his family (now with two children) to

Birkenhead, to upgrade his job with the railway board and find a new home.

When Wilfred was 14 years old his father was promoted to become Assistant Superintendent to the Joint Railways Board, affording a welcome return to Shropshire and a home in Shrewsbury. The boy picked up his education at the Technical School there well enough to impress his English teacher by his abilities in the French language and more particularly in poetry and drama, and to arouse her encouragement. The family had a fairly strict religious upbringing but for highdays and holidays they enjoyed outdoor life in Shropshire, picnicking in the 'Happy Valley' at Pontesbury with family friends, and enjoying the August fair with its noisy and colourful scenes, amusements, sports, booths and startling sideshows.

Wilfred stayed on at school until he was 18, for he was judged to be the scholarly one of the family, and that year he sat for, and passed, the London University Matriculation. Sadly, his father's job would not support a son at university, where Wilfred would have enjoyed developing his literary pursuits, and the disappointment was great. However, after a temporary and quite exacting spell of pupil teaching at Wyle Cop elementary school, the youth moved to Oxfordshire as lay assistant to the vicar of Dunsden. This proved disastrous, possibly through a conflict of faith, and Wilfred was on the verge of a breakdown when he returned home.

Following a period of illness and recuperation among various relatives, the offer of the tutoring post in Bordeaux came as a tremendous relief, the more so because Wilfred's doctor had told them that a year in the south of France was what he needed to gain strength and pull out of the bronchial troubles which had plagued him for months past. The period of successful tutoring followed, but eleven months later the blow fell. Before 1914 was out, Wilfred Owen was preparing for home.

115

By the following year his course was set. He had enlisted first in the Artists' Rifles, but on being commissioned into the Manchester Regiment he was thrown in at the deep end of the escalating conflict. He reached the Somme to see for himself the pitiless slaughter of thousands of fellow soldiers in the filth, mud and grime of the rain-sodden trenches and out on the cruel terrain where bitter winds blew upon frozen snow.

It was a horrifying experience. Though he conducted himself well the young officer fell victim to shell shock, which brought him home and to hospital in Edinburgh. The one bright spot there was his meeting with the poet — quite a hero figure to him — Siegfried Sassoon. The older man recognised and encouraged Owen's literary talent, putting his mind on course for some constructive work which was to lead to Owen's reputation as one of the greatest of the First World War poets. This was no small compliment, for at that time men of considerable literary talent were emerging, inspired perhaps by the challenging climate of the times.

Certainly Wilfred Owen's own talent deepened, as apparently did his personality. The indecisive youth had given place to a man of passion and vision arising from the depth of his feelings for the suffering witnessed. He found the power within him to express those feelings in the most potent way. Talent developed in earlier years now found purpose and direction.

Sassoon would have dearly loved to keep his young friend out of the rest of the war, which he himself deeply and vociferously deplored. But it was not to be. Owen was presumed fit to return to France for the last vital onslaught in the late summer of 1918, and once there his nerve held out. He played his part without flinching and earned for himself the Military Cross, even while, in painfully snatched moments in the billet, he was penning some of his

116

most powerful lines to include in the volume of poetry Sassoon had urged him to write.

At home in England hopes were rising that the fighting was coming to an end at last, and the news broke over the country in November with relief and joy. But on Armistice Day, of all days, as church bells were ringing all over Shropshire — and countrywide — the dreaded telegram came to 71 Monksmoor Road. Wilfred Owen had lost his life one week earlier while leading his platoon in throwing a bridge of wire-linked wooden floats across the Sambre Canal. It was an agonizing task in the face of implacable enemy fire. Most of the contingent were cut down at the waterside where a machine gun bullet picked out the small, resolute figure of their 25 year old leader and ended his life.

It is impossible to conjecture the feelings of Tom and Susan Owen that day, but they would surely have gained comfort in 1920 when Siegfried Sassoon stepped in to collate for publication the unfinished volume of poems which are now part of England's literary heritage.

'The Land Of Lost Content'

'What are those blue remembered hills,
What spires, what farms are those?'

SOME Worcestershire poets have yielded to the temptation to apply that very appealing phrase 'blue remembered hills' to the Malverns because its composer, Alfred Housman, was a Worcestershire man. But it is agreed that from the summit of the hill near his boyhood home at Fockbury, near Bromsgrove, there is a splendid view of Shropshire's Clee Hills, and later he was heard to say 'I had a sentimental feeling for Shropshire because its hills were our western horizon'. So his neighbouring county got the benefit of Housman's fame and the subsequent tourist attraction arising from his book of poems *A Shropshire Lad*. Actually the county has Housman's friend and colleague A. W. Pollard to thank for this. When given the manuscript for an opinion he advised against Housman's title *Poems by Terence Hearsay* and suggested the now famous one. Even so, the publishers MacMillan & Co refused to publish, and rather than hawk the manuscript around, Housman produced it at his own expense through Kegan Paul in 1896.

By that time Housman was in his mid thirties, a withdrawn, austere Cambridge professor who suddenly surprised his academic world by publishing a collection of

poems revealing unsuspected tenderness and a deep
sense of nostalgia. The main character featured, through
whom Housman gives voice to his own emotions, is a
21 year old ploughboy exiled from home by the call to
arms and fearing he will return no more. In retrospect
he glimpses the countryside in spring, the primrose,
the Lenten lily, the windflower, the daffodil, each
with its little span, death and joy following so quickly
the one upon the other. He hears the jingling harness,
the trampling horse, the football thudding against
the player's boot, his sweetheart's weeping farewell.
All is expressed so crisply, with superb economy
of words and syllables to construct the 63 poems of
varying length and bringing immediate impact and
expression . . .

> 'And if my foot returns no more
> To Teme nor Corve nor Severn shore,
> Luck, my lads, be with you still
> By falling stream and standing hill,
> By chiming tower and whispering tree,
> Men that made a man of me.'

It is sad to discover that a writer whose work gave so
much pleasure (despite its nostalgia) was often
overwhelmed with melancholia despite his academic
success, his outstanding wit and oratory, the pleasure of
dining with contemporaries in the beautiful Halls at
Cambridge, and the affluence which enabled him to travel
at will and become something of a gourmet.

It seems that the 'land of lost content' for him was
the childhood home where his mother died (on his twelfth
birthday) and where his father, for a time, found solace
only in solitary drinking. This was the time when he lost
all religious faith, he says, but without it he became
constantly aware of the vanity of life, and dwelt on

this theme in his writing. Nevertheless the stepmother he corresponds with regularly as 'My Dear Mamma' seems to have been a great consolation to the family and he had an excellent relationship with his brother Laurence, also a writer. His career as a Professor of Latin well satisfied him. Friendships brought comfort despite the hinted experience of a sad unrequited love which, alongside the early deaths of friends, threw shadows across his adult life.

It seems doubtful if Housman spent much time in Shropshire or got to know it well because there are some inaccuracies in his description — the well known reference to Hughley church steeple, for instance, when apparently the church never possessed one. Yet he was not troubled by this discovery on a subsequent visit, merely noting the fact and whimsically referring to a similar lapse on Matthew Arnold's part which did nothing to impair that good man's reputation or his work's popularity — and certainly Shropshire took no offence.

In 1936, 40 years after the writing of that poem, Housman's life drew to a close and his ashes were brought to Ludlow with the purpose of lodging them within the fabric of the church. This was done by injecting them through a joint in the masonry of the north wall, sealing the opening and affixing a brass plate to mark the spot. The inscription reads:

> 'Goodnight. Ensured release,
> Imperishable peace,
> Have these for yours.'

Thus Shrewsbury acknowledged its debt to him, but it would have been the verses he wrote himself a year earlier and designed for this last gathering of friends and wellwishers which left a more tender memory . . .

'O thou that from thy mansion,
    Through time and place to roam,
Dost send abroad thy children,
    And then dost call them home,

That men and tribes and nations
    And all thy hand hath made
May shelter them from sunshine
    In thine eternal shade:

We now to peace and darkness
    And earth and thee restore
Thy creature that thou madest
    And wilt cast forth no more.'

The Ride Of Wild Edric

THE extraordinary character known as Wild Edric appears to be one of Shropshire's oddest adventurers. Tales abound of his doings, both in this life and in the supernatural. He actually lived in the time of William the Conqueror and sprang to fame as the leader of the men of Shropshire against the Normans.

Even after 1066 he was not willing to accept King William, and continued to organise rebellion against him for another two years with conspicuous success. What is baffling is that later, in 1070, he came to terms with the Norman king and the circumstances point to a truce rather than a surrender. Why did the Conqueror allow him this favourable distinction? Perhaps Edric's great fighting prowess and leadership had impressed King William and he was seen a likely asset in the King's struggle against Scotland.

This is just what transpired, as Edric retained the lands which are listed as his assets in the Domesday Book of 1086. But unfortunately the man who changes sides is seldom popular, whatever the reason, so perhaps the legend which built up around him sprang from prejudice. He was supposed to be destined with his band of followers to live on for ever, haunting Shropshire's lead mines in the range of hills known as the Stiperstones.

Another version of the legend says the period of his banishment to the lead mines is to last only 'until all the wrongs of his troubled times are righted', and this has been interpreted as when Britain was to be freed from the yoke of conquerors.

Because Edric's death was never recorded as to time, place or burial, the legend gained ground, and what is also mysterious is that ultimately his possessions were confiscated by the King, just as if he had remained a traitor. No one seems to know why. Was that truce between King and rebel an uneasy one? Did rebellion flare up again? Or did the truce stipulate that Edric should retain his inheritance only for his own lifetime? If so, concealment of his death might well have been deliberate — a respite for his heirs. But records show that the King won possession in the end.

One might wonder how Edric produced any heirs seeing that legend has it he was married to a fairy! She is even named — Godda. One rather touching version of the tale is that Edric was not forced to haunt the mines at all, but that he died of a broken heart; his fairy-wife had returned home after a mysterious absence and when challenged by the angry husband she had simply disappeared! This romantic touch puts the fierce warrior in a different light.

Superstitions attached to the Stiperstones persist in all Shropshire books because of the strangely haunted atmosphere of that region. Over the years Salopians have testified to glimpsing Wild Edric and his followers galloping furiously across the wilds and many claim that mysterious knockings in the mines are the result of his appointed task — to draw attention to new lead supplies or, more importantly, to give warning whenever Britain's freedom is threatened by an enemy.

Corroboration has come from unexpected quarters. At Minsterley it was asserted by a miner and his daughter that they saw him on the eve of the outbreak of the Crimean War, and they obligingly provided a description of him! He was dark, black-eyed, with short curling hair and must have looked quite dashing in a green cloak and cap with white feather. He is said to have carried a horn and displayed a sword attached to a golden belt. These viewers were singularly favoured because their sighting confirmed the romantic touch. Edric's wife, the Lady Godda (happily reconciled in the hereafter?), rode at his side, her yellow-gold hair bound in white linen with a gold clasp.

An un-named Shropshire poet has caught the vision:

'See in the fiery sphere of nothingness
The fire-breathed soul of Edric pass apace,
Its spark enkindling in the deaden'd eye
The light of glowing iron upon his face.
There by his side rides Godda lightly borne
Upon her dappled jade, reflected emerald green
In the uncanny sheen
That glows, and pacing airy as the wind,
Scarce casting earthly sod behind,
And not a blade to bend is seen
Beneath the winged hoof!'

Others claim to have seen Edric in 1914, and again in 1939, riding in the direction from where the expected enemy would come, and so in course of time the picture of Wild Edric has changed. He is seen as a guardian of Britain's freedom — a deliverer, rather than a deserter.

Shropshire folklore attaches one other strange and apparently unconnected legend with the departed warrior. A strange fish — the biggest ever known — is said to haunt Bomere Pool which is near Edric's birthplace, Condover Hall. Around the creature's belly is strapped a sword given by Edric and all attempts to catch the fish have failed because the sword will only be yielded up when the true heirs of Condover Hall return there. They are, needless to say, supposed to be the dispossessed heirs of Wild Edric.

The Haunting of Dorothy Blount

I T has been said that death is a great leveller, but Squire Blount of Kinlet Hall refused to admit it. Class distinction was important to him in death as well as in life.

Sir George was squire of Kinlet and of Bewdley, and a very rich man by all accounts. When his curly haired young son lost his life (through choking on an apple core, alas) the squire could do no more for him than to provide a silver coffin, and the tragedy left his daughter, Dorothy, as heir to Kinlet Court with a fairly substantial fortune. Her future status then became of paramount importance to her father and he was incensed when she broke the news that she intended (in his eyes) to 'marry beneath her'. Yet she had fallen in love — not with a dashing young Romeo, as one might suppose, but with a widower named John Parslowe, a country gentleman, but untitled.

Sir George would have none of it! The worst side of his nature came into play (apparently he could be quite courteous and well controlled when it suited him) and he threatened not only to disinherit his daughter, but to return to haunt her and any children of the marriage if she persisted in her obstinacy. When the marriage did take place he made a new will, naming the issue of his sister Agnes as his heirs, and he kept up his bitter recriminations against his daughter until the end of his life.

At his death in 1581 he was given a magnificent tomb in

125

the north transept of Kinlet church with an effigy of himself kneeling alongside his wife, with their two children placed between them. A touching picture of family life! But misleading, and the aftermath makes for high drama.

A group of local women were innocently swilling their washing in a pool near the Hall when, they claimed, they were confronted by the astonishing spectacle of the squire rising out of the depths on horseback and charging straight towards them. They scattered, of course, and he disappeared. But the next appearance was still more bizarre. He was reported to have surfaced, crouched on the edge of the driving seat of his coach, furiously speeding the four horses over the grounds and through the rooms of Kinlet Hall. He then swept into the dining room and up over the dinner table where Dorothy and guests were peacefully partaking of their evening meal!

Unfortunately this was not a one off, and in time the pool was abandoned by the washerwomen and the Hall itself demolished and rebuilt. All to no avail. Still the sightings continued. Eventually the priests were called in to exorcize his restless spirit.

But what a battle they had. Each brought a lighted candle and placed it on a long oak table. Then followed the recital of a long lesson and prayers continued until all candles but one had burnt out. Alongside this they placed a flat bottle especially designed for their purpose of driving the restless spirit inside. As the last candle flame died out they concluded the proceedings, assured in their hearts that the spirit of the unforgiving father had been captured and securely stoppered in the bottle. This was then conveyed to the Blount tomb in the church, sternly warning all and sundry that it must never be removed or tampered with to ensure the peace of Kinlet Hall and the parishioners!

It seems that the bottle stayed in place for many years, but that even after it finally disappeared (and was said to contain nothing but photographic fluid) the cantankerous squire appeared no more.

Bibliography

Shropshire by Edmund Vale
A History of Shropshire by Barrie Trinder
Shropshire History Makers by Dorothy S. Wren
Legend and Folklore by John Merrell
Portrait of Shropshire by Brian J. Bailey
Shropshire and Herefordshire Villages by Geo. Haines
The Autobiography of Charles Darwin ed. Norah Barlow
Shropshire in Poem and Legend by Michael Peele, 1923
An Illustrated Literary Guide to Shropshire and
Ghostly Tales of Shropshire (by Christine McCarthy) both published by
    Shropshire Libraries.